TEACH & TOONS

50 Creative Cartoon Bible Lessons for 10–14-Year-Olds

RICK BUNDSCHUH

AND

TOM FINLEY

Youth Specialties

ZondervanPublishingHouse

Grand Rapids, Michigan

A Division of HarperCollinsPublishers

ZONDERVAN/YOUTH SPECIALTIES BOOKS

Professional Resources

Advanced Peer Counseling in Youth Groups
Called to Care
Developing Student Leaders
Feeding Your Forgotten Soul
Great Fundraising Ideas for Youth Groups
Growing Up in America
Help! I'm a Volunteer Youth Worker!
High School Ministry
How to Recruit and Train Volunteer
    Youth Workers (Previously released as
    Unsung Heroes)
Junior High Ministry (Revised Edition)
The Ministry of Nurture
Organizing Your Youth Ministry
Peer Counseling in Youth Groups
Road Trip
The Youth Minister's Survival Guide
Youth Ministry Nuts and Bolts

Discussion Starter Resources

Amazing Tension Getters
Get 'Em Talking
High School TalkSheets
Hot Talks
Junior High TalkSheets
More High School TalkSheets
More Junior High TalkSheets
Option Plays
Parent Ministry TalkSheets
Teach 'Toons
Tension Getters
Tension Getters Two

Special Needs and Issues

The Complete Missions Handbook
Divorce Recovery for Teenagers
Ideas for Social Action
Intensive Care: Helping Teenagers in Crisis
Rock Talk
Teaching the Truth About Sex
Up Close and Personal: How to Build
    Community in Your Youth Group

Youth Ministry Programming

Adventure Games
Creative Programming Ideas for
    Junior High Ministry
Creative Socials and Special Events
Good Clean Fun

Good Clean Fun, Volume 2
Great Games for City Kids
Great Ideas for Small Youth Groups
Greatest Skits on Earth
Greatest Skits on Earth, Volume 2
Holiday Ideas for Youth Groups
    (Revised Edition)
Junior High Game Nights
More Junior High Game Nights
On-Site: 40 On-Location Youth Programs
Play It! Great Games for Groups
Play It Again! More Great Games for Groups
Super Sketches for Youth Ministry
Teaching the Bible Creatively
The Youth Specialties Handbook for
    Great Camps and Retreats

4th-6th Grade Ministry

Attention Grabbers for 4th-6th Graders
4th-6th Grade TalkSheets
Great Games for 4th-6th Graders
How to Survive Middle School
Incredible Stories
More Attention Grabbers for 4th-6th Graders
More Great Games for 4th-6th Graders
More Quick and Easy Activities
    for 4th-6th Graders
Quick and Easy Activities for 4th-6th Graders
Teach 'Toons

Clip Art

ArtSource™ Volume 1–Fantastic Activities
ArtSource™ Volume 2–Borders, Symbols,
    Holidays, and Attention Getters
ArtSource™ Volume 3–Sports
ArtSource™ Volume 4–Phrases and Verses
ArtSource™ Volume 5–Amazing Oddities
    and Appalling Images
ArtSource™ Volume 6–Spiritual Topics
Youth Specialties Clip Art Book
Youth Specialties Clip Art Book, Volume 2

Video

Next Time I Fall In Love Video Curriculum
Understanding Your Teenager Video
    Curriculum
Video Spots for Junior High Game Nights

Teach 'Toons
Copyright © 1992 by Youth Specialties, Inc.

Youth Specialties Books, 1224 Greenfield Drive, El Cajon, California 92021,
are published by Zondervan Publishing House, Grand Rapids, Michigan
49530

Bundschuh, Rick, 1951-
    Teach 'Toons : 50 creative cartoon Bible lessons for 10–14-year-
olds / Rick Bundschuh and Tom Finley.
        p.   cm.
    ISBN 0-310-57541-9 (pbk.)
    Church group work with teenagers–Planning. 2. Bible—Study and
teaching (Secondary) 3. Bible—Study and teaching (Elementary)
4. Bible—Children's use. I. Finley, Tom, 1951- . II. Title
BS613.B86   1992
268' .432—dc20   92-21474
                                                            CIP

Edited by Noel Becchetti and Lory Floyd
Cover design and typography by Jamison Bell Advertising and Design
Illustrations by Rick Bundschuh and Tom Finley

Printed in the United States of America

93 94 95 96 97 98 /ML/ 10 9 8 7 6 5 4 3 2

TABLE OF CONTENTS

HOW TO USE TEACH 'TOONS

WHAT DO YOU GET when you mix cartoon art with an issue or a problem that demands a reaction? Teach 'Toons! Comic strip stories and illustrations draw students into thinking about situations they are likely to face in life, motivating them to seek practical, biblical answers.

This manual contains 50 reproducible Teach 'Toons that cover a wide variety of topics of interest to kids. Each Teach 'Toon is complete on one page—on the front is the Teach 'Toon itself, on the reverse is a simple, step-by-step lesson plan for the leader. These lesson plans are flexible. Try them for a Sunday morning Bible study, a midweek meeting, a cabin devotional, or any youth group get-together. A Teach 'Toon can be covered in 20 minutes to an hour, depending on whether you use part of a lesson or all of it. Teach 'Toons can be adapted to a handful of kids or to a house full.

Teach 'Toons from the Students' Point of View:

Students work together in small groups to read and respond to a Teach 'Toon's situation. Sometimes a Teach 'Toon is a multi-paneled story with the ending left up to the group to draw. Other times, the students discuss questions based on a full-page illustration. Some Teach 'Toons have blank dialogue balloons for the kids to fill in, while others feature fun game challenges.

Teach 'Toons from the Teacher's Point of View:

Each Teach 'Toon has a lesson plan on the back. The plans not only explain how to use the Teach 'Toons, they add suggestions for further student involvement. Creative opening activities, Bible exploration ideas, art projects, object lessons, and concluding activities are combined to communicate biblical truths with impact.

Students Discover God's Word for Themselves:

All Teach 'Toon lessons are designed to get the students into God's Word, enabling them to discover his truth for themselves. The teacher serves as a guide rather than an orator. Each lesson features an opening warm-up activity (to focus the learners' attention), a time of Bible discovery, a chance to consider application of the biblical principles, and a last step that promotes personal ownership of God's truth.

A STEP-BY-STEP GUIDE FOR USING TEACH 'TOONS:

1. Select the Teach 'Toon that will work best for your group. You know your students—the issues and troubles they face, their areas of interest, and their special needs. The 50 Teach 'Toons in this book give you plenty of ammunition in the battle for spiritual growth.

2. Read over the material yourself. You've found a lesson you like; now do the activities yourself. Make sure you understand the lesson objectives, the proper way to use the Teach 'Toon artwork, and the suggested Scriptures. Imagine yourself as one of the students. Can you think of additional ideas, activities, and Scriptures that your students would enjoy? Do all of this well in advance of class time so you will be an authority on the lesson rather than one of the learners.

3. Photocopy the Teach 'Toon art. Make enough copies of the art for your class and a few extra for visitors. The lesson plan is for your eyes only, of course, so it need not be copied. (Some people like to tuck the lesson plan into their Bibles rather than read directly from the Teach 'Toon manual during class.)

Make your Teach 'Toon copies at least a day before you plan to use them. Murphy's Law says that the church copy machine will break down the day you need a copy!

PERMISSION TO COPY: You are able to make as many copies as necessary for your class because we give you permission to do so. You may *not* make copies for the youth group across the street (nor may you accept copies from them). You must honor the copyright information printed on page 4. Thank you for your complete cooperation.

4. Have needed materials at hand. Each Teach 'Toon has a list of needed materials, including items common to any Bible study, and special materials needed for object lessons and so forth. You'll want to have sharpened pencils, erasers, Bibles, extra paper, scissors, paste or glue sticks, markers, butcher paper, chalkboard, and chalk. (In the lesson plans we assume you have a chalkboard. You may substitute a drawing pad, an overhead projector, a computerized LED display, a semaphore signal tower, or whatever serves your purpose.)

5. Make any necessary advance preparations. Each lesson plan has a section called **Before Class**. In it you'll find any instructions necessary for advance legwork. For example, a lesson may call for you to interview a church staff member. It's a good habit to check this section one week before you plan to teach the lesson.

6. Use your creativity, gifts, and insights. The Teach 'Toons and lesson plans are merely a guide. Use your own wisdom and imagination to build a valuable Bible study. After all, you know your students best!

7. Use wise teaching skills. The following are a few tips to keep in mind:

- If a topic is sensitive, you may wish to separate the guys and the girls for that lesson (guys clam up when girls are around).

- Don't seat Mr. Nitro with Mr. Glycerin.

- If possible, seat your students at tables or in circles. Chairs arranged in rows discourage discussion and involvement.

- Guide the conversation to make sure it stays on course. You want to avoid becoming sidetracked into an area that is unprofitable.

- When the kids are working in small groups, walk from group to group offering suggestions and encouragement. If you are blessed with adult assistants, seat one with each group.

- Don't let one or two students dominate the conversation. Involve shy students in the simple games and object lessons as volunteers. This will make them feel welcome and involved without putting them in an uncomfortable spotlight during discussion.

- Operate any electronic or complex equipment to be sure it's working properly. Nothing's worse than struggling for ten minutes of class time to get the VCR to play!

- Be at your class on time and ahead of your group with all of your materials ready to go.

- Take command of your class—you are the authority in charge.

- Most of all, never teach something you don't live yourself.

READING THE BIBLE FOR MYSELF

READING THE BIBLE FOR MYSELF

Main Focus: Developing a one-month commitment to private Bible reading can get kids walking with Christ.

Biblical Basis: Psalm 119:97-100; Jeremiah 23:29; John 20:31; Acts 17:11; Romans 1:16; 2 Timothy 2:15, 3:16, 17; 1 Peter 2:1-3.

Materials Needed: A copy of the Teach 'Toon for every two or three students; envelopes; pens or pencils; scratch paper; Bibles. OPTIONAL: A sheet of music.

Before Class: Photocopy the Teach 'Toon. The Teach 'Toon features 12 cards. Cut each copy of the Teach 'Toon apart and place each set of 12 cards in an envelope. Keep the original copy whole to serve as an answer sheet. OPTIONAL: If you prefer, the class could work together with you on one Teach 'Toon.

Step 1: OPTIONAL Object Lesson: Show a music sheet and ask, **Is there anyone here who could play this on a piano or other instrument?** If someone raises a hand, have the student describe how much practice and what type of knowledge it would take to play the music well. If no one responds, point out that it takes a great deal of learning and practice to play music well. It's the same with the Bible—to get to know it well takes time spent reading and practicing it.

Step 2: Distribute the Teach 'Toon envelopes to the small groups. Say, **Let's have a test to see just how much we know about the Bible. Dump out the Bible cards and put them in proper chronological order.**

When the groups are finished, reveal the proper order of the cards. Say something like, **Well, it looks like we all could use a little better understanding of the Bible. The Bible is a Christian's guide to life. It's very important that we get to know it well.**

Step 3: Distribute scratch paper and pens or pencils. Explain that to get to know the Bible well, there's no substitute for simply reading it on a regular basis. Have your students work in groups to draw a four-week calendar starting from the day's date. Each student should make his or her own copy, but the group can discuss ideas as it works.

Each person's calendar should feature the following things: the days that the student commits to read the Bible (every day or perhaps every other day), the time of day the student will read, and the amount the student will read each day. Be sure that no one bites off more than he or she can chew—ten minutes a day is a good start. You'll want to suggest a book or a long passage for students to read. Try the gospel of Mark.

Step 4: When the students have finished, have them look up as many of the **Biblical Basis** passages as time permits (list them on the chalkboard). The students are to write the significant parts of each passage somewhere on their calendars. They can paraphrase the verses.

If there is still time, ask the students to add little slogans, such as "A Verse a Day Keeps the Devil Away." Kids who like to draw can illustrate their calendars.

Encourage the young people to write down any questions they have as they read each day. You will help them find the answers.

Close in prayer.

A DEPENDABLE PAL

HERE ARE SOME CHARACTERISTICS THAT A GOOD FRIEND SHOULD HAVE. PUT A CHECK MARK IN THE BOXES THAT YOU THINK APPLY TO YOU.

☐ HONESTY

☐ CARING

☐ FUNNY

☐ CHRISTIAN

☐ GOOD LISTENER

☐ GENEROUS

☐ HELPFUL

☐ PUTS OTHERS FIRST

☐ HIGH MORAL STANDARDS

☐ STANDS UP FOR A FRIEND

☐ DOESN'T GOSSIP

☐ FORGIVING

☐ UNDERSTANDING

☐ SPENDS TIME WITH PALS

☐ LETS FRIENDS KNOW THAT THEY ARE LIKED

☐ OTHERS:

(WRITE ANY WE MISSED HERE.)

BECOMING A DEPENDABLE PAL

Main Focus: A dependable friend is a true treasure.

Biblical Basis: Proverbs 17:17.

Materials Needed: A copy of the Teach 'Toon for every student; Bibles; pens or pencils; scratch paper.

Before Class: Photocopy the Teach 'Toon.

Step 1: Ask your learners to name four things in the room we depend on. For example, we depend on chairs to hold us up. What might happen if these things didn't work as expected?

Ask, **Who can tell me some things we depend on pals for?** There will probably be a few jokes, but guide your students to come up with a list of several valid things. Write them on the chalkboard. Explain, **We depend on our friends for a lot of things. Let's talk about ways that we can become dependable friends.**

Step 2: Students can work in pairs or threes to do the Teach 'Toon, but each should have his or her own copy to fill out. After the assignment is completed, discuss the items on the Teach 'Toon, asking the students to decide which characteristic might be the most important for a friend to display.

Step 3: Hand out scratch paper. Say, **I want you to work in small groups to create a newspaper want ad for a dependable pal. In your ads, list all the qualifications you'd like to see in a best friend. You can put in a couple of funny ones if you want, but be sure to suggest at least a half dozen good things. Be sure to stress the idea of dependability; you want this friend to always be a good friend.**

Have the students describe and display their ads. Ask questions like, **Why are the things you listed important? Why is it important to be dependable? What happens when a friend isn't dependable?**

Step 4: Read Proverbs 17:17. Have your learners write this verse in their own words in light of the qualities you've been discussing.

Have each small group create a modern proverb or slogan that describes one quality of a dependable friend.

Read the paraphrased verses and the slogans. Tape the slogans to the wall for a future reminder to the students. Encourage everyone to look for opportunities this week to be good, dependable friends.

Close in prayer.

"I've Done It!"

Read the situations below. Put a check in the box of the situations that describe something you've done.

Check this box if you are totally perfect and have never made anyone mad at you → ☐ ... Liar!

WHY DID JESUS DIE FOR ME?

Main Focus: Students need to look at the crucifixion of Christ—how he died and why he died.

Biblical Basis: Mark 15; 1 Peter 2:22-24.

Materials Needed: A copy of the Teach 'Toon for each student; pens or pencils; scratch paper or index cards; tape; Bibles. Step 1 is an object lesson requiring a backpack and several very heavy objects, such as bricks or rocks. See Step 1 for an alternative suggestion. Step 5 calls for a large paper cross to be fastened to a wall or a door.

Before Class: Photocopy the Teach 'Toon. Prepare for the object lesson in Step 1, and make a paper cross as described in Step 5.

Step 1: When everyone has arrived, ask for a volunteer to come forward. (It's best to pick a small, skinny kid with a good sense of humor for this.) Place an empty backpack on the volunteer. Now reach into a box filled with heavy objects, such as bricks. Hold up a brick for all to see and say, **This represents sin. When you have sin in your life, it's like having a heavy weight on your shoulders.**

Place the brick in the backpack. Keep filling the backpack until the poor volunteer is so weighed down that he or she can hardly stand. Compare the weight of the backpack to the load of guilt and troubles that sin has placed on humanity. Ask the class, **Do you think this kid could win a marathon race wearing this pack? Could he or she run and jump and keep up with the rest of us? Why not? Well, what can this person do to take care of the problem?**

The person can get rid of the weight (which is what Christ does for the Christian), or he or she can avoid picking up the pack in the first place (sinless perfection—an impossibility). Help the volunteer out of the pack.

(If providing a backpack and bricks is difficult, simply make the volunteer carry a stack of books or other awkward items.)

Step 2: Explain, **Because of his great love for us, God's son Jesus came to earth to pay the penalty for our sin. It is he alone who can take away our burden of sin. First, I want to read the Bible's description of how Jesus died, then we'll look at why he died and why it's important to us.**

Read Mark 15 to your class or allow volunteers to read portions. To help the students follow along, you may wish to jot notes on the chalkboard. If time is short, read only Mark 15:16-41.

Step 3: Assemble the class into groups of two to four. Give each group paper and a pen or a pencil for one member to make notes. Have each group read 1 Peter 2:22-24 and answer the following questions, which you can write on the board: What did Christ do (make a list)? What did he not do? What good things happen to us as a result?

Discuss the students' findings. The good things that happen to us (we die to sin, we live for righteousness, and we are healed) answer "why" Jesus died on the cross.

Step 4: Give everyone a copy of the Teach 'Toon and a pen or a pencil. Have the students work privately to check off the areas of sin they've committed. When finished, poll the students to see if anyone was able to check no boxes at all. If your students are honest, they will have to admit they are sinners. Sinless perfection won't work for them—it's too late. The only solution is to unload the burden of sin. The answer, of course, is to give our burden of sin to Jesus. He is our only hope.

Step 5: Distribute scratch paper or index cards. Tell your students they are to work individually. Ask them to complete the following phrase: "God, forgive us when we _____." They can fill in the blank with whatever sin they feel people their age tend to trip over (lying, cheating, disrespect, shoplifting, and so forth). To avoid embarrassment, have the students list sins in a general way. However, encourage each person to privately and prayerfully think of and confess to God one specific sin he or she has committed recently.

As students leave, have them tape or tack the statements to a large paper cross that you have fastened to the wall or the door.

Church

CIRCLE ANY CARTOONS BELOW THAT SHOW WHAT THE CHURCH IS—

EYES AND EARS

Main Focus: Church is not made up of pews, sermons, and Sunday mornings. The church is Christ's body and we are the parts of it, each with a special purpose.

Biblical Basis: 1 Corinthians 12:12-20, 27.

Materials Needed: A large poster with 20 sheets of paper attached as shown (the sheets need to be thick to hide the words underneath); copies of the Teach 'Toon; Bibles; pens or pencils. Step 4 calls for markers; poster paper; scissors; paste or a glue stick. OPTIONAL: Snacks or other rewards for the winners of the game in Step 3.

Before Class: Make one copy of the Teach 'Toon for each student or pair of students. Construct a "Concentration" game as shown. Tape it to the classroom wall, but don't let anyone sneak a peek under the sheets of paper.

Step 1: Allow individuals or pairs of students to work the Teach 'Toon. Have volunteers share and explain what they circled.

The idea is for your students to learn that the church is actually the body of Christ made up of believers (see 1 Corinthians 12:27). The proper Teach 'Toon illustration to circle is the group of people with smiles. The other illustrations feature things the church *does*.

Step 2: Read and discuss 1 Corinthians 12:12-20, 27, pointing out the difference between what the passage says and the ideas on the Teach 'Toon.

Step 3: Play the "Concentration" game.

TOP

1	2	3	4	5
6	7	8	9	10
11	12	13	14	15
16	17	18	19	20

UNDER THE PAPERS

EYE	NOSE	MOUTH	HANDS	FEET
FEET	KNEES	EAR	HANDS	MOUTH
EAR	BRAIN	WARTS	EYE	SHOULDER
NOSE	KNEES	WARTS	SHOULDER	BRAIN

Divide the class into two teams. Let one player from the first team pick a number on the game. Turn that number up so that everyone can see the body part written underneath. The player then picks another number, hoping to find the matching body part. If the sheets match, tear them off and give them to the player. Alternate turns between the two teams, asking for a new volunteer each time. Decide whether team members are allowed to help or not, but make sure no one is taking notes! When the last match has been made, count the number of sheets each team has. The team with the most wins. Hand out rewards if you have any.

Tell your class, **These body parts symbolize the different functions that you and I can serve as members of Christ's body. For example, if I was like an ear, I'd be a good listener—someone who people would come to when they needed to talk about their problems. What might these other body parts represent?** Here are some suggestions: an eye—someone with insight; a nose—a person with sensitivity; a mouth—a teacher or a counselor; hands—someone who serves others; feet—someone who spreads the Gospel; a brain—a person of wisdom; knees—someone committed to prayer; shoulders—a person who carries burdens or does work; warts—this is meant to be a joke (you can discuss the dangers of always being a taker and never a giver).

Step 4: Assemble groups of three or four students, and assign each group one or more body parts. Let them draw and label the parts with a purpose as discussed in Step 3.

Have the students cut out their drawings, and paste them all together to make a cartoon poster. The results will be hilarious. The labels may have to be rearranged on the poster to fit properly.

Step 5: Encourage each student to privately and prayerfully consider what part of the body he or she might be. If any students think they are warts, tell them to talk to you after class. Pray with them for a remedy to change their warts into functioning body parts.

Close in prayer.

IMAGES OF... DAD!

MATCH THE VERSES WITH THE IMAGES OF GOD'S FATHERLY LOVE THAT THEY DESCRIBE.

OUR FATHER

Main Focus: God is our loving Father.

Biblical Basis: Psalm 34:4, 68:5, 119:12, 147:3; Matthew 6:4, 7:11; John 10:15; Romans 8:15; Hebrews 12:6; James 1:17; 1 John 3:1; 2 John 4.

Materials Needed: A copy of the Teach Toon for every student; pens or pencils; scratch paper; Bibles; small reward for Step 1. Step 3 calls for 8 1/2 x 11 card stock and colored felt pens.

Before Class: Photocopy the Teach Toon.

Step 1: Write the word *Abba* on the chalkboard. Pass out a slip of paper and a pencil for each student to write what he or she thinks the word means. Toss a small reward to those who correctly say the word means "Daddy."

Say something like, **Today we are going to look at the idea of God being our loving Father. If your dad wasn't around much or if he was a poor example for you to follow, this might be difficult for you to picture, but God gives us an example of perfect fatherhood.**

Step 2: Pass out a copy of the Teach Toon, a pencil, and a Bible to each student. Ask the students to match the description of God with the verses given.

Have the kids describe what they discovered about God's nature as a loving Father. The discoveries should include that God instructs us as a father teaches a child, delivers us from fear just like a father's presence makes a child feel secure, tenderly treats our wounds and sadness just like our physical parents do, becomes the father to the fatherless, adopts us into his family, sometimes makes us take a "time out" for our correction, gives us good gifts, and willingly gave his life for us just as a human father would for his child.

You may wish to point out that not everyone can call God "Father." The right to claim that relationship belongs to those who have put their trust in God's most perfect gift—Jesus Christ.

Step 3: Distribute 8 1/2 x 11 card stock and colored felt pens. Ask each student to create a Father's Day card for the heavenly Father. Encourage the kids to seriously consider what they would like to say to God in their cards.

Step 4: Ask your students to share their cards and then collect them to place in the offering plate as a gift to God, or hang them around the classroom.

Close in a prayer of thankfulness for God's love and care.

SETTING A GOOD EXAMPLE

HERE'S A FUN GAME! THE CARDS BELOW ARE DIVIDED INTO SETS OF THREE. EACH SET SPELLS OUT SOMETHING THAT WOULD BE A GOOD EXAMPLE FOR OTHERS TO FOLLOW. ONCE YOU'VE READ THE CARDS, CUT THEM OUT AND SHUFFLE ALL THE #1 CARDS INTO A PILE, ALL THE #2 CARDS INTO A PILE AND ALL THE #3 CARDS INTO A PILE.

NOW DRAW A #1, #2 AND #3 CARD TO FORM A NEW SENTENCE. IS IT A GOOD EXAMPLE? TRY AGAIN WITH ALL THE CARDS.

#1	#2	#3	#1	#2	#3
I NEVER	PICK	MY NOSE IN PUBLIC.	I WANT TO	MEMORIZE	MY BIBLE FROM COVER TO COVER.

#1	#2	#3	#1	#2	#3
I ALWAYS	WEAR	WARM CLOTHES IN WINTER.	IT'S GOOD TO	RETURN	WHATEVER YOU'VE BORROWED.

#1	#2	#3	#1	#2	#3
I TRY TO	EAT	HEALTHY FOOD.	YOU SHOULD	PAMPER	YOUR PETS.

#1	#2	#3	#1	#2	#3
I LIKE TO	BRUSH	MY TEETH AFTER EVERY MEAL.	DON'T	KICK	INNOCENT ANIMALS.

SETTING A GOOD EXAMPLE

Main Focus: Christians need to set good examples for others to follow.

Biblical Basis: 2 Chronicles 27:2; Matthew 5:16, 38-44; Titus 2:3-5; 1 Peter 2:12.

Materials Needed: A copy of the Teach 'Toon and a pair of scissors for every two or three students; pens or pencils; index cards; scratch paper; Bibles.

Before Class: Photocopy the Teach 'Toon. Make cards as described in Step 1.

Step 1: Write the following phrases on index cards, one phrase per card: giving flowers to little sister, helping someone pick up dropped books, turning down a drink and a smoke, telling a friend about God, helping an old person to cross the street.

Each phrase represents a situation that student volunteers are to act out. To begin, call a pair of volunteers to the front of the class. Give them a card and instruct them to silently act out the phrase while the other students try to guess what they are watching. No props can be used. (Give volunteers a few seconds to plan their actions.) Do this for all five cards, calling new volunteers each time. Drop a few hints, if needed, to help the class guess each action.

Thank everyone and say, **What were these people doing? They were setting good examples. They were performing kind acts, avoiding temptation, sharing the Gospel. You might not realize it, but each of you is an example to the people who watch you. Are you a good or a bad example for your friends and loved ones?**

Step 2: Give each group of two or three students a Teach 'Toon and a pair of scissors. Have the students read the sentences before cutting them up and rearranging them to form silly examples. This step is mostly for fun, but it's a good lead-in to the next step.

Step 3: Brainstorm a list of the types of behavior Christian kids should exhibit. Ask your students to suggest ten or more good examples they could set in a typical day, and write them on the chalkboard. Ask, **What do you suppose people would think about you if you were consistently a good example of a Christian kid? Would you have more friends at school or less? Would they be better friends or worse? What might God think and do?**

Step 4: Assign the **Biblical Basis** passages (except Matthew 5:38-44) to small groups. Allow a few minutes for the students to study and discuss their passages. They should look for at least one principle involved in trying to set a good example.

Discuss the groups' findings. In 2 Chronicles 27:2, we learn that not everyone will respond to godly behavior. Matthew 5:16 says that Christians do have an important impact on this generation. Titus 2:3-5 makes the connection between teaching by word and teaching by example. First Peter 2:12 confirms that good deeds will glorify God.

Read Matthew 5:38-44. Point out that Jesus not only told us to do all these things, he also set the example for us by his death on the cross. He even prayed for the people who were killing him (see Luke 23:34).

Step 5: Point out that setting a good example for others is much like being a signpost on a highway that people read and follow. Have the students draw signs giving important advice about setting good examples, and hang them around the room.

Close in prayer.

AND THE WINNER IS...

LOOK AT THE DRAWINGS ON THE LEFT. READ THE BIBLE PASSAGE WITH EACH, THEN DRAW A LINE TO THE APPROPRIATE "WINNING EVENT" ON THE RIGHT. AN EXAMPLE HAS BEEN DONE FOR YOU.

SUCCESS OR FAILURE?

Main Focus: *A man's own folly ruins his life, yet his heart rages against the Lord* (Proverbs 19:3). Kids can be angry inside—blaming God for their failures. This lesson discusses God's blueprint for success.

Biblical Basis: Selected verses from Proverbs.

Materials Needed: Scratch paper; Bibles; pens or pencils; a copy of the Teach 'Toon for each small group of students; a chart on the chalkboard as shown in Step 3. OPTIONAL: A target, a dart gun with rubber-tipped darts, and rewards as described in Step 4.

Before Class: Photocopy the Teach 'Toon. To save class time, write the chart in Step 3 on the chalkboard. If you are doing the optional game in Step 4, draw a target as shown.

Step 1: Try folding a sheet of paper in half, then in half again and so on eight times. It's impossible! Demonstrate this with a sheet of scratch paper or newsprint. Distribute scratch paper to the students and challenge them to try. When everyone gives up, say, **Like it or not, some things are beyond our ability to do. Life is like that. We don't always get what we want, and we are not always as successful as we'd like to be. Sometimes people blame God for their own failures or for their "lot in life." Today we're going to look at what makes a person successful in God's eyes and how we can achieve that success.**

Step 2: Give a copy of the Teach 'Toon and a Bible to each group of two or three students. Allow the students several minutes to complete the assignment. Have volunteers describe their answers.

Step 3: Write the "Qualities of Success and Failure" chart shown below on the chalkboard.

PASSAGE	QUALITY OF SUCCESS?	ANY BENEFIT	QUALITY OF FAILURE?	ANY DEFICIT
PRO. 10:7 12:3 13:5 16:3 17:27,28 22:4 25:27 26:24-26 28:12 28:13				

Have a volunteer read the first verse, Proverbs 10:7. Ask the class if there is a quality of success mentioned in the verse and, if so, what is the benefit of practicing that quality. (The quality is righteousness and the benefit is being a blessing to others.) Guide the students to see the quality of failure (wickedness) and the deficit (a rotten name). Be sure to explain any biblical terms the kids might not understand. Follow these steps for all the verses.

Step 4: Ask the students to suggest areas in life where kids tend to fail (home, school, with friends, and so forth), and write them on the chalkboard. Encourage the students to suggest specific ways practicing the qualities of success (and failure) might affect the way a kid relates to people at home, in school, and in the other areas.

OPTIONAL: To make this step fun, play this exciting game. Make a target like the one shown. Let your students take turns shooting at it with a dart gun or spit wads or marshmallows. If a student misses, he or she sits down. If a question area is hit, ask the student to tell how one of the qualities of success (your choice) could positively affect how a person relates to people at home, in school, and so on. If the answer is a good one, give the student a soda, candy, or other reward. You'll find your whole class involved in this one!

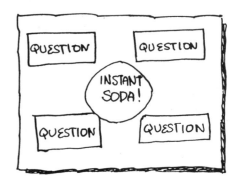

Step 5: Close in prayer, asking each student to think of at least one area of success he or she will practice this week.

THE STORY OF SLOW JOE

WRITE A SHORT STORY ABOUT A GUY WHO KEEPS COOL IN "HOT" SITUATIONS. THEN, CUT OUT AND GLUE ANY PICTURES YOU NEED TO HELP WITH YOUR STORY. DRAW ANY OTHER ILLUSTRATIONS TO THE STORY WITH A BLACK FELT PEN.

PATIENCE—
THE "SLOW JOE" METHOD

Main Focus: Be quick to hear, slow to speak, and slow to anger.

Biblical Basis: James 1:19-27.

Materials Needed: Bibles; a copy of the Teach 'Toon and a pair of scissors for every student; pens or pencils; paste or glue sticks; paper; a paper cutter; a stapler.

Before Class: Cut 8 1/2 x 11 plain paper sheets into thirds using a cutting board. (Cut the 11-inch side at a little over 3 1/2-inch intervals.) Cut one sheet for each student. Fold the three paper strips in half, put them together, and staple them in the center as shown. Assemble a mini book for each student.

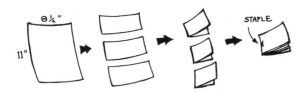

Step 1: Ask your students to share with each other the last time they got into trouble for losing their tempers or shooting off their mouths.

Say, **As you can tell from your own experience and that of your friends, we often get into hot water because we are so quick to talk or to become angry. Let's get some practical insight from the Bible about this problem.**

Step 2: Give each student a copy of the Teach 'Toon, along with a mini book, glue, and a pen or a pencil. Instruct your students to read James 1:19-27, then ask them to create the story of "Slow Joe" based on the prescription from the Bible. Students select pictures from the Teach 'Toon, glue the art in place, and add their text to the bottom of each illustration.

When finished, ask volunteers to read their stories.

Step 3: On blank pieces of paper, have the students work privately to finish the following sentences for their own lives. (Assure them that you will not read these or share them with the group.)

If I was quick to hear, I would . . .

If I was slow to speak, I would . . .

If I was slow to get angry, I would . . .

Close in prayer.

WHAT'S THE DIFFERENCE?

LOOK UP THE VERSES ON THIS PAGE AND DECIDE IF THEY MATCH THE NEW NATURE CHRIST HAS GIVEN YOU OR THE OLD EVIL NATURE YOU WERE BORN WITH. THEN DRAW A LINE TO THE BODY PART DESCRIBED AND TELL WHAT IT DOES. (SEE EXAMPLE)

ECCLESIASTES 8:1

ISAIAH 59:3

MATTHEW 6:3
DOESN'T KNOW WHAT THE RIGHT HAND IS DOING

1 TIMOTHY 1:5

ROMANS 3:15

PHILIPPIANS 3:19

PROVERBS 27:20

OLD NATURE

JEREMIAH 17:9

ROMANS 10:15

LUKE 21:18

JEREMIAH 7:26

NEW NATURE

OLD NATURE/NEW NATURE

Main Focus: Christ wants to change us from what we are to what we can be.

Biblical Basis: Proverbs 15:7, 27:20; Ecclesiastes 8:1; Isaiah 22:12, 59:3; Jeremiah 7:26, 17:9; Matthew 6:3; Mark 15:19; Luke 21:18; John 9:10, 11; Romans 3:15, 10:15, 11:10; 2 Corinthians 5:17; Ephesians 4:23; Philippians 3:19; 1 Timothy 1:5.

Materials Needed: A copy of the Teach Toon for each student; pens or pencils; scratch paper; Bibles; pictures as described in **Before Class**. OPTIONAL: An obituary and a birth certificate as described in Step 3.

Before Class: Find a number of "before-and-after" pictures in a magazine (before-and-after weight loss, makeup job, and so on).

Step 1: Hang the before-and-after pictures around the meeting room. Have the students vote on which is the most drastic improvement. Say something like, **We are going to look at another before-and-after job—the one that God is doing on us by trying to remake us in his image.**

Step 2: Read 2 Corinthians 5:17 and Ephesians 4:23 to your class. Ask your students to explain how a person gets a new nature from God.

Hand out the Teach Toons. Have the students look up the verses written on the cartoon and match the examples with the drawings that fit best. (If time is short, have the kids work in pairs to look up the verses—one starting at the top of the list and the other at the bottom.)

Some examples of the old sinful nature of mankind are a stiff neck (a proud spirit), a person who worships his or her appetite, fingers stained with guilt, a deceitful heart, and a mind that is never satisfied.

In contrast, the new nature that Christ places in us shows up figuratively in a pure heart, eyes that can see, feet that bring good news, lips that spread knowledge, and wisdom that brightens the countenance.

Point out the contrast between what our old nature offers and what the new nature through Christ promises.

Display the finished work on the wall.

Step 3: Remind your students that God asks us to get rid of or to "put to death" our old nature and to become a new person in Christ. With that in mind, ask the students to create obituaries or tombstones for their old natures and/or birth certificates for their new natures. (You may want to bring a sample obituary and birth certificate to show your group.)

When the class members are finished, have them share what they have created. Post their work around the classroom.

Step 4: Have each student write down on paper one area of his or her old nature that should be "buried." You can even symbolize the death of these areas by burying the sheets of paper.

Close in prayer, asking each person to pray silently regarding the area he or she wants to bury.

Grave Comments

THE PEOPLE BURIED IN THIS CEMETERY WERE VERY POETIC. THEY ALSO HAD A LOT OF **DOUBTS**. YOU CAN SEE WHAT THEY DOUBTED—AND HAVE SOME FUN AT THE SAME TIME—BY COMPLETING THE POEMS.

MY DAD WAS A BACKSEAT DRIVER, HE'D SWEAT WHEN I WOULD DRIVE; HE'D SAY, "I KNOW WE'RE GOING TO CRASH, I DOUBT WE'LL STAY _____ ."

DAD

I LOVE CLIMBING UP THIS GIANT MOUNTAIN WALL. AND THOUGH I FORGOT MY SAFETY ROPE, I DOUBT THAT I WILL _____

"I DON'T BELIEVE IN DENTISTS AND I DON'T BRUSH ANYWAY."

(THAT'S WHY THIS FOOLISH PERSON UP AND DIED OF
- TOOTH _____)

YO, BABY—
YO BABY, YO—
YO, I LOVE TO SMOKE; CANCER AIN'T NOTHING, BABY— I DOUBT I'LL EVER _____

I DOUBT ANYONE WILL READ MY GRAVESTONE, IT'S JUST HO-HUM; BESIDES, I DOUBT IF I'LL THINK OF A RHYME TO FINISH THIS _____

I DOUBT SANTA. I DOUBT THE EASTER BUNNY. I DON'T BELIEVE IN THE TOOTH FAIRY. I SCOFF AT THE BOOGIE MAN. I'M NOT SCARED BY SPOOKY THINGS—I JUST DON'T CARE ABOUT IT.

MY FRIENDS SAY I MUST DOUBT EVERYTHING. BUT I SAY,
"I _____ !"

No Doubt!

Main Focus: Everyone has doubts now and then, but doubts must not be allowed to fester. Here are some ways to find answers to doubts.

Biblical Basis: Matthew 11:1-6; 1 John 3:24.

Materials Needed: Copies of the Teach 'Toon; Bibles; pens or pencils.

Before Class: Photocopy one Teach 'Toon for every two or three students. Consider the evidences of God's reality (Step 3) and think of specific examples of answered prayer, miracles, transformed lives, and so forth. Be ready to relate these to your class during Step 4.

Step 1: Allow your students to work in pairs or threes to complete the Teach 'Toon. Have volunteers read their completed poems. Ask students to describe a few of the things they tend to doubt. What do they think are the differences between questioning, doubting, and disbelief?

Say, **Believe it or not, many of the great saints of the Bible went through periods of questioning and doubting. Today we'll look at one of them, a guy named John the Baptist. His example is a good one to follow when we have questions and experience doubt about God.**

Step 2: Present a little background on John the Baptist. He helped pave the way for Christ's appearance by preaching about the coming Messiah. Thousands listened to him and believed, repenting of their sins. He was thrown in jail for accusing King Herod of shameful behavior. Although John had strongly believed that Jesus was the Messiah, he began to doubt as he wallowed in prison.

Read Matthew 11:1-6. Ask your students to suggest answers to the following questions: **Why do you suppose John started to doubt? What did he do when he felt doubts? Who did he go to in order to resolve his doubts? Who should we go to when we start to doubt?**

Step 3: Put God on trial—is he real? Conduct a trial, letting volunteers suggest evidences for his reality. These evidences should include the accuracy and self-consistency of the Bible, the testimony of an intricately designed creation, miracles, changed lives, answered prayer, and the witness of the Holy Spirit (1 John 3:24). Suggest any of these that the kids don't think of and expound on the significance of each.

Tell the students that these evidences work together to wipe out doubts. Point out that people who know the Bible well, who talk to God often in prayer, who carefully consider the evidence of creation, who listen to mature Christians and otherwise wrestle with these evidences for God's reality tend to have their doubts and questions answered. On the other hand, people who leave their Bibles on the shelf and disregard the other sources of verification of God's reality are often defeated by their doubts.

These same principles apply to people who have doubts about their salvation, God's love for them, the existence of the Devil, and so on.

Step 4: On the chalkboard, list all the categories of evidence that you discussed. Ask the students to think of specific examples of as many of these evidences as they can. For example, do they know anyone whose life has been radically transformed by God? Can they tell about a miracle? Have they seen any answered prayer? Give your own examples.

Encourage the kids to privately examine their own hearts to see if doubts linger. Offer your ear to anyone who wants to talk after the class.

Close in prayer.

IF I WAS ~~WIZE~~
WERE — WISE

READ THROUGH EACH SITUATION BELOW. IN THE MIDDLE PANEL, DRAW WHAT YOU THINK WOULD BE THE WISEST (BEST, MOST RIGHT) THING TO DO. THEN ANSWER THE QUESTIONS.

I'M BAILING OUT OF SCHOOL! I CAN'T KEEP UP WITH SMART GUYS LIKE YOU!

1. HOW DO "SMART GUYS" IN SCHOOL GET THAT WAY?

2. WHY IS IT WISE TO BE SMART?

I'M SO MISERABLE! SNIFF! MOM AND I HAD A FIGHT! I WANT TO RUN AWAY!

1. HOW COULD READING THE BIBLE HELP AN ANGRY, HURTING PERSON?

2. WHAT WOULD YOU DO IF YOU DIDN'T KNOW HOW TO FIND SOME HELPFUL VERSES FOR THAT PERSON?

HEY! ME AND DANNY ARE GONNA SWIPE A COUPLE OF CDs! KEEP AN EYE ON THE CLERK FOR US!

1. WHY IS IT UNWISE TO STEAL?

2. WHAT DOES BEING A CHRISTIAN HAVE TO DO WITH WISE LIVING?

WISE UP!

Main Focus: God and his Word will help us become wise people.

Biblical Basis: Proverbs 3:1-4, 5-10, 13, 14; 4:5-9, 10-13; Matthew 2:1-12.

Materials Needed: One copy of the Teach 'Toon for each pair of students; pens or pencils; large markers; writing paper; Bibles; two large sheets of poster paper.

Before Class: Photocopy the Teach 'Toon. Prepare two posters: Write "The Wise Person is…" at the top of one and "Benefits of Wisdom…" at the top of the other. Fasten the posters to the wall.

Step 1: To help your students focus on the idea that God and his Word are the sources of wisdom, say, **I want you to tell me some sources of things. What is the source of the electricity that powers our lights? What is a river's source? What is the source of bread? What about a head cold? What's the source of wisdom?** Explain that the Bible is our source for true wisdom to live by.

Step 2: Read aloud or have the students read sections of the story of the Magi (see Matthew 2:1-12). Tell your students, **The Magi have traditionally been called the wise men. From what you've read, why do you suppose they've been labeled as wise?** Lead a discussion, helping the students to arrive at the following insights. In verse 1, they came seeking the Messiah, something wise people still do. In verse 2, they knew of a special star either through a divine revelation or through solid knowledge of the Old Testament (see Numbers 24:17). Verses 2, 10, and 11 show that they came to worship—they had faith. Verse 12 tells us they were wise enough to listen to and obey God's instructions. Write the following on the chalkboard: Seek the Truth, Study the Bible, Have Faith in God, Listen to God, Obey Him.

Step 3: Assemble your students into groups of three or four, and distribute writing paper and pens or pencils. Assign each group one of the following passages from Proverbs: 3:1-4; 3:5-10; 3:13, 14; 4:5-9; and 4:10-13 (you can double up assignments or skip some to allow for the size of your class). Say, **I want you to search your passage for two things. First, look for phrases that seem to match any of the things on the chalkboard. Note these on your paper. Then look for any benefits of doing the things recommended in your passage. List these on your paper and be ready to discuss them with the class.**

Discuss the groups' findings.

Step 4: Distribute copies of the Teach 'Toon to groups of two or three students. Have them complete the cartoon situations and answer the questions. Discuss how the Bible's instructions regarding wisdom relate to the day-to-day situations a student is likely to face.

Step 5: Pass out markers and ask the kids to fill out the posters on the wall with important principles they've learned, then close in prayer.

30

1. WHAT CAN THE NEW KID DO TO CHANGE HIS NOSE?
   ☐ NOTHING
   ☐ WEAR A MASK
   ☐ _____

2. WHAT COULD YOU SAY AND DO TO HELP HIM OUT?

   ◉

   ◉

   ◉

I Feel Like a Leper!

Main Focus: A person's value is not based on physical appearance.

Biblical Basis: Leviticus 13:45, 46; 1 Samuel 16:7; Matthew 8:1-3.

Materials Needed: A copy of the Teach 'Toon for every two people; pencils or pens. From a fashion magazine, cut out a large photo of a "beautiful person." Also, try to find a photo of a homeless person, perhaps from a news magazine.

Step 1: Leviticus 13:45, 46 tells us that in biblical times people with any type of infectious skin disease (such as leprosy) were singled out from society. They lived alone outside the community. When they did come though town, they had to shout, "Unclean, unclean." They also had to dress shabbily as a sign of grief for their separation from Israel.

Describe to your students these Levitical rules regarding the treatment of lepers, or have the students work in small groups to research the passage and list the rules. Discuss the nature of a leper's life—rejection, humiliation, and loneliness.

Step 2: Read Matthew 8:1-3 aloud. When you read verse 2, ask your class to describe what the leper had probably gone through in his life, based on the Leviticus passage. How was he most likely dressed? What sort of place would he have lived in? How was he most likely treated by people?

That last question is the most important, for it leads the discussion toward the way Jesus treated the man. Unlike everyone else, Jesus touched him. He reached out and welcomed the man. Jesus associated with him. This contact allowed the miracle of healing.

Step 3: Have your learners work in pairs to complete the Teach 'Toon. It's the story of a kid who is ridiculed for his big nose. When the assignment is completed, have the students suggest other things that might cause a kid to be rejected by peers—not just physical features, but also types of behavior and so forth. Finally, discuss (or have small groups discuss) how Jesus might have treated the boy with the big nose.

Tell your class that it seems as though every school has at least one luckless kid who is treated like a leper. It may be because the kid is very ugly or strange or weak. By now, your students will be pointing to each other! Point out that kids probably mocked the lepers in times past. Ask your students how they would feel to be a leper in those conditions.

Step 4: Read the last part of 1 Samuel 16:7: *"The Lord does not look at the things man looks at. Man looks at the outward appearance, but the Lord looks at the heart."* Working with your students, make a list of several things that the Lord might honor in a person (honesty, concern for others, kindness).

Step 5: Show the pictures of the gorgeous person and the homeless person. How would the world tend to value each? How should a Christian value each?

Jesus touched and healed the leper. What are some practical ways a young Christian could reach out to a "school leper?" How might the concern a Christian shows help to heal a lonely person? Close the session in prayer.

LIAR, LUNATIC, OR Lord of all?

Read the Bible passages, draw a simple picture illustrating what happened, and fill in the questions.

MATTHEW 9:2-8

Did the teachers think Jesus was a blasphemous liar, crazy fool or the Lord God?

MARK 3:20-21

When they found that he was not eating, Jesus' family thought he was _____.

JOHN 20:26-29 (This took place after Jesus rose from the grave.)

Thomas thought Jesus was _____.

Who do YOU think he is?

33

IS JESUS GOD?

Main Focus: Sooner or later most youth workers find that their young people are being confronted on campus by kids who deny that Jesus is God. These kids are often members of cults and seem (to young Christians) to know what they are talking about. Here is some ammunition for your response.

Biblical Basis: Isaiah 9:6, 44:6, 8; Matthew 4:10, 28:9; Mark 2:5, 7; Luke 7:48; John 1:1, 3, 14, 5:18, 9:38, 10:30-33, 14:6-9, 20:27, 28; Philippians 2:5-11; Colossians 1:16, 17; Titus 2:13; Hebrews 1:3, 8.

Materials Needed: A copy of the Teach 'Toon for every two or three students; pens or pencils; poster paper; Bibles; index cards. OPTIONAL: Since your class will conduct a trial as explained in Step 2, you might wish to wear a judicial looking robe and carry a gavel. See Step 1 for optional materials.

Before Class: Photocopy the Teach 'Toon. Prepare ten index cards as described in Step 2.

Step 1: Assemble your class into groups of two or three students. Give each group a copy of the Teach 'Toon and a pen or a pencil. The assignment calls for a little artwork on the part of your students. If some complain they have no talent, encourage them to draw stick figures. OPTIONAL: Allow the kids to use ink pads to make thumbprints on the Teach 'Toon. They can draw arms, legs, hair, and the like on the thumbprints to serve as the artwork.

When done, ask the students (rhetorically), **Who do you think he is—liar, lunatic, or Lord of All? Let's take a look at the evidence we find in the Bible.**

Step 2: Prepare ten index cards to be read by student "witnesses" who present the verses listed on the cards as evidence in a trial your class will conduct. The trial is to determine if Jesus is truly God. The references for each card are listed below. Be sure to write the number (1 though 10) on each card because they will be presented in order at the trial.

1. John 14:9, 10
2. John 5:18, 10:30-33
3. Isaiah 9:6; John 1:1, 14; Titus 2:13
4. Isaiah 44:6, 8; Exodus 20:3; Matthew 4:10; Matthew 28:9; John 9:38
5. John 20:27, 28
6. Mark 2:5-7; Luke 7:48
7. Genesis 1:1; John 1:3; Colossians 1:16, 17
8. Hebrews 1:8
9. Hebrews 1:3
10. Philippians 2:5-7

Distribute a card or cards to each group. Have the students look up the references and select one or more group members to read the passages aloud during the trial.

At the beginning of the trial, explain, **I am the attorney on behalf of the Lord Jesus. I will call witnesses to present evidence. When I call your card number, come take the witness stand, and read your passages. I might ask you some questions or I might point out the significance of the evidence myself.**

The significance of the passages on the cards is as follows: (1) Jesus claimed that seeing him was the same as seeing the Father; (2) Jesus made himself equal to God and never denied it when so accused; (3) The Bible calls him God; (4) Both the Father and the Son make it clear there is only one God and only he is to be worshiped, yet Jesus allowed himself to be worshiped; (5) Jesus allowed himself to be called God; (6) Jesus forgave sins, something only God can do; (7) God and Jesus are both described as the Creator of everything; (8) God the Father calls Jesus God; (9) Jesus is the exact representation of God; and (10) Jesus is in very nature God.

Point out that to deny that Jesus is truly God, one must deny the Bible. Serving as judge, declare that the evidence overwhelmingly proves that Jesus is indeed God.

Step 3: Have each group take its card and create a small poster that describes the significance of the passages. Hang the posters on the wall to serve as a reminder that Jesus is truly God.

Close in prayer.

Say What?

Each situation below has really happened. Read each cartoon, then write your responses in the two dialogue balloons.

BAD RESPONSE:

GOOD RESPONSE:

DID YOU HEAR? JUSTIN HAS **DRUGS** IN HIS LOCKER. AT LEAST THAT'S WHAT AMY SAYS...

BAD RESPONSE:

GOOD RESPONSE:

HEATHER'S BEEN OUT OF SCHOOL ALL WEEK! WANT TO GUESS WHAT I'VE HEARD? IT'S JUICY!

BAD RESPONSE:

GOOD RESPONSE:

CHECK THIS OUT! IT'S A **LOVE LETTER** FROM KYLE THE DORK!

GOSSIP

Main Focus: Words can build up or destroy a friendship.

Biblical Basis: John 2:1-11; Ephesians 4:29; selected verses from Proverbs.

Materials Needed: Paper and markers to create a tabloid-style newspaper; Bibles; pens or pencils; one copy of the Teach 'Toon for each pair of students. Prepare index cards or paper with the Scripture assignments used in Step 3.

OPTIONAL: A lurid grocery store tabloid to show your students as an example of a gossip sheet; large prescription bottles filled with little candies (the bottles can be obtained from a friendly pharmacist at very little cost); tape.

Before Class: Photocopy the Teach 'Toon and prepare the Proverbs cards.

Step 1: You can start the lesson by playing the old gossip game—one student reads Proverbs 17:9 silently, closes the Bible, and attempts to whisper the verse word for word to a neighbor. The verse is passed along until the last kid in class hears it and repeats it aloud. It will be distorted and perhaps garbled, illustrating the dangers of passing along gossip.

Step 2: Form groups of three or four students, giving each group the material necessary to make the front page of an imaginary gossip tabloid (show the class a real one if you have it). Explain that you want each group to make a gossip sheet based on the story of Jesus changing the water into wine (see John 2:1-11). Some kids can draw "photographs" for the paper, while others write headlines or simple stories. The point is to distort the story of Jesus' miracle—make it look like the party was a drunken brawl, Jesus was promoting alcoholism, and so on. Tell your students to write down anything they can think of that would distort what actually happened.

Be sure your learners understand that they are not to ridicule or trivialize the Scripture passage. Instead, they are to take a serious look at one of the Devil's tricks—gossip—and the damage it can do.

When finished, display the papers and ask the students to describe what they created. Ask questions like, **If stories like these had really been circulated, what harm might have been done to Jesus and his ministry here on earth? Would it have been hard for Jesus to correct the lies? What might he have to do to straighten everything out—or could he? What are some things students tend to gossip about? What sort of damage can these stories do?**

Step 3: Distribute writing paper and the Proverbs passages, one card per group. One group gets Proverbs 10:19, 11:13, and 15:28. Another gets Proverbs 10:32, 12:18, and 21:23. The third group gets Proverbs 16:24 and 17:9, and the last gets Proverbs 20:19 and 26:20. (These cards contain just the references; you needn't write out the passages.) If you have a small class, give two or more cards to each group or assign fewer passages overall. Large classes can work on duplicate assignments. Say, **Stay in your same groups for this. First, read the verses I'm giving to you. Then create a label for a prescription bottle. The label contains a list of ingredients for preventing gossip. Base your ingredients on what you read in the Bible.**

When complete, display the labels and discuss what has been learned. If you have the optional prescription bottles, have the students tape the labels to the bottles and enjoy the candy.

Step 4: Let your groups work on the Teach 'Toon assignment. When finished, discuss these situations or any others that may be of concern to your students. Help your students understand how the biblical advice they studied can be of practical importance in daily interaction.

Step 5: Allow the students to work individually to read and paraphrase Ephesians 4:29. Ask each person to prayerfully think of something to say to a friend that would benefit and build up that person.

Close in prayer.

FAMILY LIFE

Circle the situations that happen pretty often in your house. Be honest — no one will see this paper but you.

THE ONE THING I WILL DO THIS WEEK TO SHOW A SPECIAL KINDNESS
TO _____ IS: _____.

Can We Talk?

Main Focus: Communication is a key to family happiness.

Biblical Basis: Mark 3:20, 21; Luke 2:41-52; John 19:25-27.

Materials Needed: A copy of the Teach 'Toon for each student; pens or pencils; Bibles.

Before Class: Photocopy the Teach 'Toon.

Step 1: Give your kids a fun challenge to focus their attention on today's subject. Explain, **I'm going to read five sentences to you, each containing the word** *stink*. **It's your job to figure out the real word I'm looking for.** Read the first sentence in the next paragraph. Allow one or two students to guess the word, which is *communicate*. Read as many clues as it takes until a winner is found.

(1) We use the telephone to stink. (2) We stink when we talk to each other. (3) Families need to stink. Mine does. (4) I want to stink with you today. If I do, you'll learn important things. (5) To stink means to exchange information.

If no one has guessed the word, reveal it. Say something like, **It's very important for every member of a family to communicate. Communication is the bridge that helps a family remain healthy. If the bridge is down, trouble happens.**

Step 2: Give a copy of the Teach 'Toon and a pen or a pencil to each student. Give the kids a few minutes to complete the assignment, then tell them to put the Teach 'Toons away in their pockets, purses, or Bibles.

Without asking students to reveal specific negative family situations, discuss the sort of problems typical families can experience. Ask questions like, **How many minutes a day do you think the average kid has a real conversation with his or her folks? Do most brothers and sisters your age get along well? What are some things that make it hard to communicate with parents or siblings?**

Ask your young people if they think Jesus ever had trouble communicating with his parents. He did—or, at least, they did with him.

Step 3: Have volunteers read Mark 3:20-22 and Luke 2:41-52. In the first passage, Jesus drew large crowds and drove out demons. As a result, his family thought he had turned into a crazy fanatic. They misunderstood who he was and what he was doing. In the second passage, Jesus was left behind, probably because of his age. At 12 years old, he could travel in the front of the long caravan with his mom, the women, and the children. But he was also old enough to travel at the rear with his dad and the other men. It's likely that Joseph thought Mary had him and vice versa. Mary frantically looked for her little boy, not quite willing to recognize he had grown up into a responsible young man.

Before pointing out that Jesus returned with his parents and lived under their authority for probably another 18 years (according to some Bible scholars), spend a good amount of time discussing why the misunderstandings happened in these two passages and how they might be similar to what kids experience at home today.

Step 4: Tell students, **I want you to stand up. Stand against the left wall if you think family life would be better at home if your nose grew two inches every time you told any kind of lie. Stand against the right wall if you think family life would be better if you could get away with lies.**

Ask several students to explain why they made the choices they did. The point here is that honest communication would require strict obedience to mom and dad's rules. Is it better to do that or to gain a little freedom by disobeying some rules? Lead your students to understand the correct response. Point out that Jesus obeyed his parents despite the personal freedoms it may have curtailed.

Step 5: Read John 19:25-27. This passage portrays Christ's concern for his mom even while he suffered on the cross. Ask the students to write on their Teach 'Toons one thing they will do this week to show a special kindness to a family member.

Close in prayer.

IMPORTANT NOTE: Let the kids know you are available to meet with them privately if they want to talk more about specific family problems. Be prepared, however, for the possibility that one or more of your students may reveal incidents of physical and/or sexual abuse, drug and/or alcohol abuse, or other problems that you are legally obligated to report to the proper authorities and qualified counselors and therapists in your area.

WHAT WOULD YOU DO?

Look at each situation. Check off what you'd really do

1. You can work for the Lord at an inner-city mission this summer

OR

You can relax and get a good tan

- [ ] WORK FOR THE LORD
- [ ] TAN

2. IF YOU COULD HAVE A **DATE** WITH ANYONE, WHO WOULD YOU CHOOSE?

- [ ] THE BIGGEST HUNK OR FOX IN SCHOOL
- [ ] THE KID WHO LOVES GOD THE MOST

(DISREGARD THIS QUESTION IF THE BIGGEST HUNK OR FOX IS ALSO THE BEST CHRISTIAN!)

3. WE NEED YOUR HELP WITH THE YOUTH GROUP PARTY TONIGHT!

YOU CAN GO NEXT TIME. LET'S GO TO THE MOVIES.

- [ ] YOUTH GROUP
- [ ] MOVIES

4. YOUR BEST FRIEND DRIVES A BICYCLE. A NEW KID WANTS TO BE YOUR BEST FRIEND. HE DRIVES A CAR. WHO IS YOUR BEST FRIEND GOING TO BE?

- [ ] GOOD OL' BEST FRIEND
- [ ] NEW KID

5. Matthew 6:24b says:

"YOU CANNOT SERVE BOTH GOD AND MONEY."

AT THIS POINT IN YOUR LIFE, WHAT DO YOU WANT MOST?

- [ ] GOD
- [ ] MONEY

6. PUT THE FOLLOWING THINGS IN ORDER OF IMPORTANCE **TO YOU** (1 BEING BEST).

- [ ] LOTS OF BUCKS
- [ ] HEALTH
- [ ] BIBLE KNOWLEDGE
- [ ] GOOD LOOKS
- [ ] NEW PARENTS!

I Want It All

Main Focus: Kids are materialists, but God wants nothing to stand between us and him.

Biblical Basis: 1 Samuel 2:7; Matthew 4:8-10, 6:19-21, 24; Mark 8:34-36; Colossians 3:2, 3.

Materials Needed: A copy of the Teach 'Toon for each student; pens or pencils; scratch paper; Bibles; index cards prepared as described in **Before Class**. Step 4 calls for magazines; glue sticks or paste; markers; scissors; poster boards.

Before Class: Photocopy the Teach 'Toon. Prepare five index cards, printing one phrase per card:

> Own a totally hot car
> Have super rock star talent
> Win a fabulous shopping spree
> Win a huge lottery
> Become a champion skateboarder (substitute whatever sport is most popular with your class)

Step 1: Pick five volunteers to help you. Give each person one of the prepared index cards. Explain to the volunteers and the class that the cards feature things kids would like to own, win, or do.

One at a time, the volunteers are to silently act out the phrases on the cards while the class attempts to guess what they're about. Allow a few moments for preparation. Let the volunteers select kids from the class to help pantomime their phrases.

Congratulate the performers and the students who guessed the phrases. Explain, **This was a fun way to kick off today's study, which focuses on materialism. What is materialism? It is the sinful practice of valuing things more than we value God. Keep in mind that while having nice things, being rich, and achieving fame is not necessarily bad, it is if these things divert our attention from God, the one who really matters.**

Step 2: Distribute one copy of the Teach 'Toon to each student, along with a pen or a pencil. Say, **This is a materialism test. Although tongue in cheek, it does have a serious purpose. As you answer the questions, it is very important that you answer honestly. Check off what you think you would actually do, not what you think I would want you to do. No one will look at your paper but you.**

Allow several minutes for the students to work, then review the Teach 'Toon by asking volunteers to describe how their peers might respond to each situation.

Step 3: List the **Biblical Basis** references on the chalkboard (except 1 Samuel 2:7). Assign the passages to groups of three or four students. Each group is to summarize its passage (or passages) on scratch paper and prepare to explain it to the class.

Discuss each passage, probing for information regarding a Christian's attitude toward material things.

Step 4: Keep the students in their same groups. Give them the materials necessary to create posters featuring material things cut from magazines—things that the world desires and longs after. Your students are to label the posters with advice and slogans based on the Scriptures studied.

Display the results.

Step 5: Give each group time to review and paraphrase 1 Samuel 2:7. Lead a discussion based on the important truths of the passage. How do these truths relate to today's study? Does this passage motivate a shift in our attitudes toward material things? What hope does the passage give to people who have little? Is it wiser to base our lives on material things or on God? Why?

Close in prayer.

CUT IT OUT

Use this artwork to make a "Maturity Manual" based on the Bible passages and marks of maturity you've looked at today. Draw additional cartoons yourself. Add words and Bible verses. Make the manual in such a way that your friends could read and understand it.

GROWIN' UP Manual! BY THE KIDS AT:

BIBLE

SPEECH

WISDOM

MOM & DAD

STATURE

1 TON STRENGTH

IMMATURITY

GOOD REPUTATION

GROWING UP

Main Focus: The Bible lists things your students should strive for as they reach for maturity.

Biblical Basis: Matthew 21:28-31; Luke 2:51, 52; 1 Timothy 4:12; Titus 2:6.

Materials Needed: A copy of the Teach 'Toon for every two or three students; pens or pencils; scratch paper; scissors; paste; Bibles; a stapler. You'll need index cards filled out as described in **Before Class.** OPTIONAL: Candy or sodas for the winning group in Step 1.

Before Class: Photocopy the Teach 'Toon. Scramble the following words and write each on an index card: *bragging, blabbing, dishonesty, mooching, fighting, silliness, irresponsibility, cheating,* and *thoughtlessness.* (You can scramble just a few letters of each word if you have a younger class or scramble each word thoroughly if you have a class full of geniuses.) If you have a large class, make multiple copies of each scrambled word. Hide the cards in fairly obvious places around the classroom or, weather permitting, outside.

Step 1: Tell the students to search the room in pairs or threes to find the index cards. When they find one, they are to decode it and continue the search for others. After a few minutes, call time and see who has had the most success. You may wish to hand out a small reward to each member of the winning team or teams.

List the words on the chalkboard and say, **Can anyone tell me what these words are a sign of? They are a sign of immaturity. Anyone who does these things needs to grow up. Whether you are 13 or 63, if you do these things, you are immature. Today we want to talk about growing up and what God says about it.**

Discuss each word at length. (*Blabbing* refers to gossiping or the inability to keep a secret.) Have the students suggest examples of each behavior that kids tend to see in others or do themselves.

Step 2: Read and discuss in turn each of the **Biblical Basis** passages. List on the chalkboard all the terms the students can find that are marks of maturity. Examples include obedience to parents, wisdom, physical stature, a good image in the eyes of God and friends, self-control, good speech, good lifestyle, love, faith, purity, and—in the case of Matthew 21:28-31—doing the right thing even when it's distasteful.

Step 3: This Teach 'Toon is a bit different from the others. It is clip art for making a "Growin' Up Manual." Give each group a Teach 'Toon, scissors, paste, and several sheets of paper. Each group makes a multi-page manual that features the cartoon art (and any they'd like to draw themselves) and tips from the Bible passages. The manuals should show examples of signs of both immaturity and maturity. Each cartoon should have a descriptive caption. The last page of the manual could feature a summary list of things to do to become a mature person.

Staple the pages to form the manuals. As time permits, allow several groups to show and explain their manuals. Thank everyone for their efforts.

Step 4: Encourage your students to prayerfully search their own hearts for signs of maturity.

Close in prayer.

FIND THE DEADLY FORM OF PRIDE

CIRCLE ALL OF THE CASES OF SPIRITUAL PRIDE (THINKING YOU'RE A BETTER PERSON THAN SOMEONE ELSE) YOU CAN FIND ... BUT BE CAREFUL, NOT ALL THAT LOOKS LIKE PRIDE REALLY IS.

THE POISON OF PRIDE

Main Focus: Pride is thinking I'm a better person than you!

Biblical Basis: Romans 12:3; Galatians 6:3.

Materials Needed: A copy of the Teach 'Toon for every two or three students; pens or pencils; a large marker; scratch paper; a large sheet of paper; Bibles.

Before Class: Photocopy the Teach 'Toon. Tape a large sheet of paper to your meeting room wall. In the middle of the paper, write the word *Pride*.

Step 1: As your kids enter the meeting room, have them use a marker to write their ideas of what pride is on the paper.

Introduce the subject to the class by reading a number of the comments. Explain, **You have given some thoughtful ideas to the meaning of *pride*. Today we are going to take a look at the kind of pride that is deadly to our Christian lives and to our function as decent human beings.**

Step 2: List the **Biblical Basis** Scriptures on the chalkboard. Hand out paper and pencils. Have your students write in their own words the definition of dangerous pride that is described in the passages.

Ask volunteers to share what they have written. Make sure they understand what makes spiritual pride (thinking oneself better than others) so deadly. It's okay to be pleased with talent or accomplishment, but when these things result in feelings of superiority, that's evil. Ask the following questions: **Is it a bad kind of pride to be happy because your team wins a tournament? What could make it a bad kind of pride? Is there anything wrong with knowing and acknowledging that you are good at a particular thing? Under what conditions would this turn into a deadly form of pride?**

Step 3: Distribute copies of the Teach 'Toon to groups of two or three students, and ask your class to locate as many forms of deadly pride as it can. Caution the kids not to confuse pride with satisfaction of achievement.

When the time is up, discuss the various situations they have located. What makes them prideful? Ask, **Are any of these situations similar to what happens in real life? How do you feel when someone acts egotistical and vain? What do people think of a person who does this?**

Step 4: Ask the students to sum up the main idea of the lesson by writing a prescription for spiritual poison, complete with the skull and crossbones warning sign. For example: DANGER! Poison to your soul! Contents: one part egotism, two parts "I think I'm so hot," a drop of "I know everything," and a cup of "I'm a much better person than you are."

Display the prescriptions. Close the lesson in prayer.

WHAT IS GOD LIKE?

★ FOLD OVER TO MAKE ARROWS MEET....

TRUE · GOOD
MIGHTY ·
ETERNAL ·
POWERFUL
CARING · LORD
TRUSTWORTHY
LOVELY
GRACIOUS ·
THE SAVIOR

AND A LOT MORE !!

JESUS SHOWS US GOD

Main Focus: We learn what God is like by looking at his son Jesus.

Biblical Basis: Mark 2:9-12, 5:35-42; John 1:14, 10:28; Hebrews 1:3.

Materials Needed: A copy of the Teach 'Toon for every two or three students; pens or pencils; scratch paper; poster paper; markers; Bibles; a potato "dressed up" as described in **Before Class.** OPTIONAL: Candy and sodas for Step 4.

Before Class: Photocopy the Teach 'Toon. Make a potato look human (like the old "Mr. Potatohead" game) by using stiff paper to create the eyes, a nose, a mouth, ears, glasses, and whatnot. Let your imagination loose on this one. Use tacks or toothpicks to attach things to the potato.

Step 1: To start things off, assemble small groups. Have each small group fold their Teach 'Toon. The words should form the word *Jesus.* List the words from the Teach 'Toon on a blackboard. Ask the students to explain why they think Jesus is a good representation of God the Father. When the discussion is over, move to Step 2 by saying, **I want to show you why it's important to realize that Jesus is more than just a man who had some of the characteristics of God. Take a look at this . . .**

Step 2: Pull out Mr. Potato so everyone can get a good look. To liven things up you can do a few jokes, using your own voice and the squeaky voice of Mr. Potato.

Explain, **Mr. Potato is trying to pass himself off as a human being. I suppose he looks sort of like a human—well, not really. He might fool another potato, but none of us in this room is stupid enough to think Mr. Potato is anything like a real person. To really show us the traits of a human being, Mr. Potato would have to be fully human. The Bible says that Jesus is the exact representation of God. His traits and behavior here on earth showed us exactly what God the Father is like. But in order to do that, Jesus couldn't be just a human being dressed up like God— he had to be God.**

Let's look at a few of the things that Jesus taught us about God the Father.

Step 3: Write the **Biblical Basis** Scriptures on the chalkboard (except for Hebrews 1:3). Gather your students together into groups of three or four. Distribute materials necessary for each group to make a wanted poster. Explain that the person wanted on the poster is not a crook, but Jesus Christ. But like a real wanted poster, this one is to feature a description of Christ's characteristics (as found in the Scriptures).

Your students will find the following characteristics: Christ has miraculous power and forgives sin (Mark 2:9-12); he shows compassion and raises the dead (Mark 5:35-42); he is God and he is eternal (John 1:1— explain that the rest of John 1 makes it clear that this verse is speaking of Jesus); and he gives eternal life (John 10:28).

Display the wanted posters and discuss Christ's characteristics. Point out Hebrews 1:3: *The Son is the radiance of God's glory and the exact representation of his being. . . .* Thus, Christ's traits are God's traits. We know that God is compassionate, eternal, powerful, and all the rest because that's what Christ is like.

Step 4: Take everything off your Mr. Potato, being careful to remove all tacks and toothpicks. Gather everyone into a circle. Say, **I'm going to toss this potato to someone and he or she must toss it quickly (but safely) to another. It's a hot potato. At my signal, anyone touching the potato must answer a question. Anyone who holds the potato too long will have to answer a question.**

This is a fun way to wrap up the class with discussion. Base your questions on the characteristics of God and Christ listed on your wanted posters. Ask questions like the following: **How might the characteristic of compassion be of value today—on campus, in the home, and with friends in the youth group? Why is the characteristic of healing important in a believer's life? Which of God's characteristics can Christians also have and which can't they have? What are some ways a Christian can demonstrate these traits?**

If your kids are not quick to respond to questions, try plying them with candy and sodas as rewards.

Close in prayer.

DISHONESTY AND DIRTY DEEDS

Main Focus: God wants us to be upright in all of our actions.

Biblical Basis: Leviticus 6:2-5; Psalm 37:21; Proverbs 11:1; 1 Thessalonians 4:6; 1 Peter 3:10.

Materials Needed: A copy of the Teach 'Toon for each student; Bibles; pencils or pens; paper; envelopes; stamps.

Before Class: Photocopy the Teach 'Toon.

Step 1: Try an activity we call "Voting With My Feet." Have the students stand in the middle of the room. Read aloud the following situations. Have the students move to the right or to the left of the room in response. Everyone must make a choice; there can be no one in the middle of the room after each vote. (Have everyone return to the middle of the room before each vote.)

1. You find out that the young doctor who is scheduled to perform a minor operation on you cheated on tests in medical school. Move to the right if you would allow him or her to perform the operation. Move to the left if you would change doctors.

2. Your girlfriend or boyfriend lies to his or her parents when caught in a pinch. Do you think he or she will be likely to lie to you? Move to the left if no or to the right if yes.

3. A friend who used to say, "Sometimes you have to tell a few tall tales to get ahead" now sells cars. Would you buy a car from that friend? If your answer is no, move to the left. If your answer is yes, then move to the right.

Invite your students to discuss their feelings on the situations. Say something like, **It is clear that dishonesty is not a trait that many of us admire or would like to see practiced on us. But it is not an uncommon problem. Let's check the Bible for a better idea of where a person might turn a corner into dishonesty.**

Step 2: Have your students work in pairs or threes. Hand out paper and pens or pencils. Ask everyone to look up the passages listed under **Biblical Basis.** Each group is to create a crossword puzzle out of the various kinds of dishonesty exposed in the passages, including the verses to support what it lists. You may wish to give the example shown above to help everyone understand this activity.

Have the groups share what they have discovered.

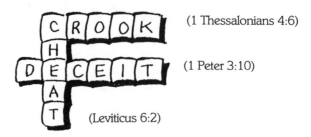

(1 Thessalonians 4:6)

(1 Peter 3:10)

(Leviticus 6:2)

Step 3: Distribute a copy of the Teach 'Toon to each person. Everyone should take a look at the situations pictured and draw appropriate responses.

Encourage your class members to consider honestly what they would do if they found themselves in these situations.

Step 4: Pass out paper and envelopes for everyone to write a self-addressed letter as a reminder to be honest and truthful in the areas each is struggling with at the moment. Do not ask to read the letters.

Collect the sealed letters and close in prayer. A month or so later, stamp and mail the letters back to the students.

LET'S PARTY!

PARTIES ARE GREAT PLACES TO HAVE FUN! BUT SOME PEOPLE DON'T KNOW HOW TO HAVE **REAL** FUN. LOOK AT THE PEOPLE BELOW. WHICH DO YOU THINK ARE HAVING REAL FUN? WHICH ARE NOT? IN THE SQUARES, WRITE WHAT YOU THINK COULD HAPPEN TO THE PEOPLE IN EACH SITUATION.

LET'S PARTY!

Main Focus: Jesus liked to go to parties and so do the members of your youth group. This session allows your students to discuss the nature of fun and celebration. They will plan a youth group party.

Biblical Basis: Matthew 22:1, 2; Luke 5:29-34; John 2:1-10.

Materials Needed: A copy of the Teach 'Toon for every two or three students; pens or pencils; scratch paper; Bibles; materials to make party invitations; refreshments and decorations or party favors for a class party.

Before Class: Photocopy the Teach 'Toon. Prepare the room for the party.

Step 1: Welcome everyone to your class party. Serve the refreshments and any party favors you have. Explain, **Today we want to take a look at partying! Did you know that Jesus liked to party? He sure did. In fact, the Gospels recount several parties that he attended.**

Tell your students to enjoy their refreshments while they work in small groups to complete the Teach 'Toon. When finished, discuss the situations on the Teach 'Toon. Who is having fun? Who isn't? Why?

Step 2: Read Matthew 22:1, 2 aloud. Tell your learners that wedding banquets in those days were week-long affairs that featured constant partying, music, food, fun, and celebration. They were major blowouts! Jesus compared heaven to this sort of party. Not only has God set up heaven as a wonderful party, his son Jesus liked to attend parties here on earth.

Have the students follow along as you read about the wedding at Cana in John 2:1-10. Point out that this was the very first miracle that Jesus performed in public. He was at a party, socializing with friends and neighbors, when the wine ran out. Running out of wine would have been a great humiliation to the family throwing the party. Jesus used his miraculous powers to keep the party going.

Luke 5:29-34 describes another party Jesus attended. Again, the nature of the party was one of celebration and feasting. Make it clear to your students that Jesus loves to have fun and wants us to have fun, too.

Step 3: The important thing to discuss now is the nature of fun. Christians can enjoy true fun—good, clean fun—or they can partake in the seamier so-called fun of intoxication, lewdness, and so forth. (Some students may wonder if this miracle justifies intoxication. Be sure to point out that drunkenness was not a part of this party. Also, it's clear that Christians must obey the laws of the land. Children drinking wine is not justified by the events of the passage.)

Perhaps the greatest difference between Christian fun and worldly fun is the results. Christian fun builds people up and makes them feel good. Worldly fun can be damaging or cause conflicts and, in the end, usually makes a person feel guilty.

Step 4: Let your kids plan a youth group celebration. Pick a date, decide on a reason (anything from a parent appreciation party to an after-the-big-game celebration), and plan the events (music, food, and games). Assign various responsibilities to volunteers—who'll bring the CDs, what types of food each person should bring, who will decorate, and so on. Encourage the students to make this party their party—they can make it as fun as they like as long as they put in the energy and effort. If you are not the senior youth worker at your church, work with him or her during or after class time to finalize the plans.

Step 5: Give the students the materials necessary to make party invitations. Small groups should make enough invitations for all the people they would like to invite. Students can distribute the cards at the appropriate date (you may wish to collect the cards until then).

Close in prayer, thanking God for the great fun that Christians can enjoy.

SOMETHING IS FISHY

READ THE STATEMENTS BEING MADE IN VARIOUS SITUATIONS. THEN READ THE BIBLE PASSAGE LISTED, AND DESCRIBE HOW THAT PASSAGE RESPONDS TO THE STATEMENT.

CULT CITY

Main Focus: Kids need to understand the difference between true Christianity and various cults.

Biblical Basis: Isaiah 45:5; Matthew 25:31-34; Luke 24:39; John 1:1-3, 14:6; Romans 3:10-12; Ephesians 2:8, 9.

Materials Needed: Play money; Bibles; butcher paper; felt pens; a copy of the Teach 'Toon for every two or three students.

Before Class: Photocopy the Teach 'Toon. Buy some play money at a toy store to use for the opening exercise.

Step 1: Start your class by showing play money and asking students to explain the similarities between play money and the real thing. They should mention that both are made of paper, they look similar, and they both have a value printed on them. There are two main differences: one has the authority of the government behind it, while the other does not; one will buy things, while the other will not.

Point out the similarities between phony money and cults. Both imitate the real thing but are void of true authority.

Step 2: Distribute the Teach 'Toons to small groups. Ask the students to respond to each of the statements made. Have them look up the passage suggested under each cartoon for the true Christian response.

The essential ideas covered in the Teach 'Toon are as follows:

- There is only one God; we can never be him. False religions claim that someday we can become gods or merge into God.

- Hell is a real destination for unbelievers. God loved people so much that he came to earth and died so that people would not have to end up there. As unpopular as the idea may be, hell is taught by the Bible.

- Christ is the only way to God—sincerity doesn't count. The Bible does speak to the problem of people who have never heard about Christ (see Romans 2 for the principle), and we can be sure of God's ultimate fairness. Yet it is true that all those who will be saved will owe it to the shedding of Christ's blood.

- The Bible clearly teaches that people are basically evil. Modern myth teaches that people are basically good. Tell that to the millions killed by Adolf Hitler in World War II.

- Jesus is God incarnate, God in the flesh. He is part of the triune God made up of Father, Son, and Holy Spirit. He was not a "sub-god" or an elevated angel.

- Jesus rose from the dead in a physical form. He could be touched, and he could eat. Any attempt to reduce the wonder of the resurrection is the mark of a counterfeit.

When ready, let several volunteers describe their results.

Step 3: Using the orthodox Christian doctrine discovered by completing the Teach 'Toon and any other Scripture or creeds you wish to introduce, have your class members create a "We believe . . ." statement. Write it with a felt pen on a large piece of butcher paper.

Step 4: Encourage everyone to respond to the statement they created by signing the document if they intend to hold to its ideas.

Close in prayer.

THE LOOK ON HIS FACE

READ MATTHEW 14:22-33 AND DRAW THE EXPRESSIONS THAT YOU THINK PETER'S FACE MIGHT HAVE HAD DURING THIS ADVENTURE!

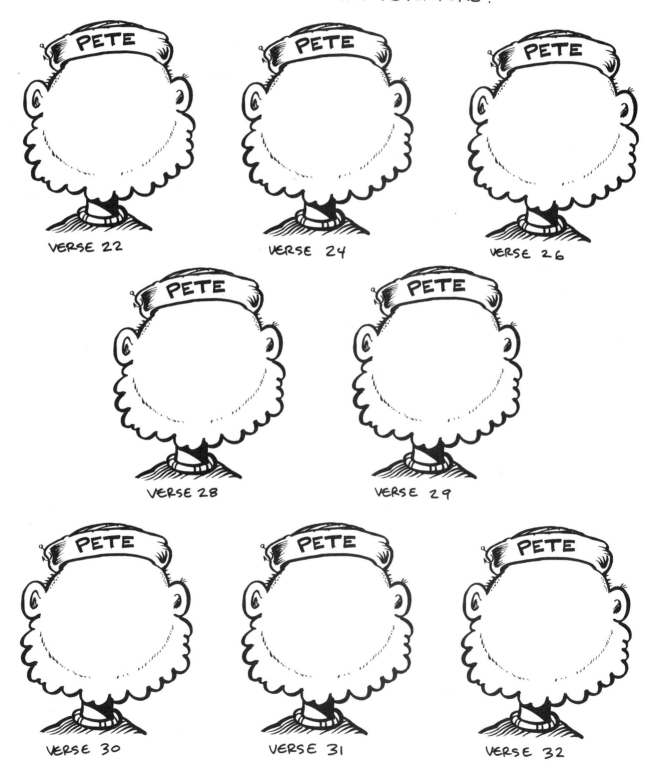

VERSE 22

VERSE 24

VERSE 26

VERSE 28

VERSE 29

VERSE 30

VERSE 31

VERSE 32

STEPPING OUT IN FAITH

Main Focus: We must trust God in spite of our circumstances.

Biblical Basis: Psalm 23; Matthew 14:22-33.

Materials Needed: A copy of the Teach 'Toon for each student; pens or pencils; scratch paper; Bibles; several mousetraps; a blindfold.

Before Class: Photocopy the Teach 'Toon. Recruit a couple of students to help you with a special trick you will play during the class (see Step 1). Set the mousetraps and put them out of sight until you're ready to use them.

Step 1: Spread several mousetraps across the floor. Ask for one volunteer to trust you to guide him or her safely through the mine field of mousetraps. Have your volunteer remove his or her shoes and put on a blindfold. Stand on the opposite side of the mine field from the volunteer and begin to give directions: forward, stop, two steps left, one step forward, and so forth. What your volunteer does not know is that as soon as the blindfold was put on, a couple of students in cahoots with you silently slipped all of the mousetraps out of the way.

Talk to your students about the nature of trust. The volunteer trusted that you would not lead him or her to harm. The student listened to your voice and instruction.

Step 2: Distribute the Teach 'Toons and pens or pencils to the group. Read Matthew 14:22-33 or ask volunteers to read it in sections. Have the students work on the Teach 'Toon, drawing what they think Peter's facial expressions might have shown during this experience. Your students may need to have their imaginations challenged to come up with some good expressions. One way is to have a volunteer try to take on the expressions as they are called out by the class. Kids can use these as a model to draw from.

Discuss the adventure Peter had by asking the following questions: **Who do you think was smarter, Peter or the other guys in the boat? What do you think Peter's fishermen friends on the shore would have said if he came back and told them that he had been hiking on the lake? If you were Peter, what one lesson would be branded into your mind?**

When finished with the expressions, allow the students to show what they have done.

Step 3: Divide your students into groups of three or four. Have each group create a short, narrated skit or pantomime that shows a situation where faith would be hard for a teenager to employ. For example, a kid is told by his parents that they do not approve of him being so involved in all the "religious stuff." Or perhaps all of the kids on a team are unbelievers—they put subtle pressure on the one Christian team member to compromise her faith by lying, disobeying her parents, or smoking.

Have the groups perform their skits for the entire class.

Step 4: Read Psalm 23 as students prayerfully consider any areas of their lives where trusting God in difficult circumstances is a struggle.

Close in prayer.

WHAT'S THE PROBLEM HERE?

READ JAMES 1:27, 2:14-20. WHAT IS THE PROBLEM WITH EACH OF THESE SITUATIONS? HOW MIGHT A CHRISTIAN RESPOND?

WHAT ABOUT THE DOWN AND OUT?

Main Focus: Christians need to give with compassion.

Biblical Basis: James 1:27, 2:14-20.

Materials Needed: Bibles; pencils; paper; a copy of the Teach 'Toon for each learner. NOTE: You may wish to have material available from various relief organizations, such as World Vision, Compassion International, and World Relief, for students to take home or fill out.

Before Class: Photocopy the Teach 'Toon.

Step 1: Read the following story to your class:

> Charlie Steed couldn't believe it at first. The numbers for the big lottery prize were being read on the TV and they matched his ticket. He was three million dollars richer! Charlie had been scraping by on his meager salary as a night watchman.
>
> The phone rang off the hook. Friends and relatives called up to congratulate him. But a funny change was happening to Charlie. Each of those phone calls seemed to be a subtle hint for a piece of the pie. Charlie quickly figured out that if he cut all of his friends a piece of that three-million-dollar pie, it would quickly be gone. So he decided to keep it all for himself. Let them win their own lotteries!
>
> One cold and crisp autumn day Charlie drove his shiny new Mercedes down East Main Street. He noticed the dented and rusty heap that belonged to his best friend, James, was stalled on the shoulder of the road with the hood up. Huddled inside were James's wife and three kids. Then Charlie heard his name being called. James was crossing the street and fast approaching the driver's window.
>
> James popped his head into the beautiful interior. Softly reminding Charlie that he had never before asked him for anything, he requested a small loan to get a decent car for the family.
>
> Charlie peered straight ahead. Without a word, he pressed the close button on the automatic window. His friend quickly jumped away, and Charlie drove into the brisk morning without ever looking back.

Ask your students, **What do you think of Charlie? What would you have done? Would you ask your best friend for help if you were in James's situation? Was Charlie under a moral obligation to help his best friend?**

Step 2: Direct your students to James 1:27 and 2:14-20. Have them list on scratch paper what they see as the main ideas of these passages. Then have them discuss their insights with one another.

Step 3: Distribute a copy of the Teach 'Toon to each student. Have the kids write down what problems they see in the illustration, based on the verses studied.

Step 4: Ask your class members to brainstorm what they could do to make a difference in the lives of people represented by the TEACH 'TOON situations.

Have the students privately write down one way they could use what they have more compassionately. Distribute any materials you have from relief organizations, allowing the students a chance to review them or to fill out anything that applies.

Close in prayer.

~PETER POPS IN AND OUT OF PRISON~

REARRANGE THE CARTOONS TO CORRECTLY DESCRIBE THE ADVENTURE OF PETER RECORDED IN ACTS 12:1-19. ADD ANY DIALOGUE NEEDED UNDER EACH PANEL.

JAMES BEHEADED BY COMMAND OF HEROD (VERSE 2)

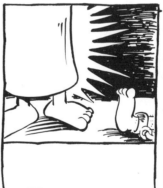

YOU CAN'T STOP GOD!

Main Focus: God is bigger than any problem.

Biblical Basis: Acts 12:1-19.

Materials Needed: Bibles; pencils; scissors; glue sticks or rubber cement; scratch paper; a copy of the Teach 'Toon for every two or three students.

Before Class: Photocopy the Teach 'Toon.

Step 1: Write the word *Problems* on the chalkboard. As your students enter the room, hand them a piece of chalk and ask them to write down one problem that kids their age must deal with.

Acknowledge that the problems stated are genuine, and make a move to the next part of the lesson by saying, **During this meeting we will be exploring an incident from the history of the early church that reminds us God is bigger than any of our problems.**

Step 2: Distribute copies of the Teach 'Toon, pencils, Bibles, scissors, paper, and rubber cement or glue sticks to groups of two or three students. Tell everyone to read Acts 12:1-19. They are to cut and rearrange the Teach 'Toon in the correct order, filling in the dialogue balloons for the story as they go.

Note the irony of Peter's adventure: God's action was much larger than what Peter or the members of the praying church expected. Peter assumed that he was dreaming about his escape from prison. He went along in a sleepwalking manner until the event was over. Likewise, the members of the church were praying fervently that God would intervene on Peter's behalf—and they were astounded when he did! Some thought Peter had been killed and that it was a ghost knocking on the front door. God is indeed bigger than our expectations and troubles.

You may wish to stimulate discussion by asking, **Why do you think that God saved Peter but let James, the brother of John, be killed?**

After your students have finished rearranging the story in the correct order, check and post their finished work.

Step 3: Hand out scratch paper, and ask the students to create a prayer for a kid in a tough spot. The problems brainstormed in Step 1 can provide some good ideas.

Have various students read their prayers. Ask questions like the following: **Do you think God answers "fire escape" type of prayers from those who only want to get out of trouble? Why or why not? Do you think God ever allows the people he loves to go through terrible events? If so, what could be some of the reasons for this? What do you think is the key attribute that Peter displayed during his time in prison?**

Step 4: Ask your students to rewrite their prayers for their own tough spots. Do not read these. Have the students silently pray their prayers in closing.

IMAGINE HEAVEN!

THEN DRAW AT LEAST ONE ILLUSTRATION SHOWING WHAT HEAVEN COULD BE LIKE.

BEYOND YOUR WILDEST DREAMS

Main Focus: Heaven is the place to be!

Biblical Basis: Matthew 6:20; John 10:28, 14:2; Revelation 21:10-25.

Materials Needed: Bibles; pencils; paper; index cards; marking pens; cartoons or photos showing ideas of heaven; poster board; a copy of the Teach 'Toon for each student.

Before Class: Photocopy the Teach 'Toon. During the week collect images of what people picture heaven to be like. The images you find should have the typical ideas of clouds, winged angels, harps, and pearly gates. An old family Bible with color plates is a good source for this sort of illustration. Display the Bible art and put other images on a poster board in the meeting room.

Step 1: As the class members enter the room, direct their attention to the images of heaven. Students should give their opinions of the likelihood that heaven will be as pictured. You will probably get mostly negative responses.

Tell your learners, **It is impossible to really know what heaven will be like, but we can get a small glimpse from the descriptive symbols used in the Bible.**

Step 2: List on the chalkboard the passages from the **Biblical Basis** section. Write the following instructions: If the passage describes heaven symbolically, what possible idea might it represent? If it suggests a condition of life, what do you think it means? For example, streets paved in gold might be symbolic of overwhelming beauty and majesty.

Assemble groups of three or four students. Pass out pencils and paper to each group. Ask the class members to look up the passages and record every idea and suggestion about heaven they can find. Point out the difficulty a human has in viewing heaven and then putting the sight in understandable words. It's almost like asking a fish in the sea to tour Disneyland and then describe the place to his finny friends!

When ready, have volunteers describe what they have discovered.

Step 3: Distribute a Teach 'Toon to each student. Have the kids draw their concepts of heaven, combining what they've just learned with their own imaginative ideas.

Show what the students come up with. Explain to your kids that we don't truly know what heaven will be like, but we can catch enough of a glimpse to know that we will really like it!

Step 4: Give each learner an index card. Explain that heaven is God's desired destination for everyone, but some choose not to go there. They are like people who pass up a personal invitation from God to join him in paradise. With that in mind, ask everyone to work individually to create an "admission ticket" to heaven. Make sure that it expresses what it takes to enter, what it costs, and who pays the price of admission. Tell your students to put their names on their tickets if they wish to receive God's gift to them. Post the tickets around the room, then close in prayer.

Time Well Spent?

STUDY THE CARTOON. WRITE NEXT TO EACH ONE WHAT FOLLOWING LETTERS APPLY (NOTE: SOMETIMES MORE THAN ONE LETTER CAN APPLY) <u>A</u> = A TOTAL WASTE OF TIME <u>B</u> = USUALLY TIME WASTED <u>C</u> = A FAIR USE OF TIME <u>D</u> = A GOOD USE OF TIME <u>E</u> = HOW I USE MY TIME

THE GIFT OF TIME

Main Focus: Time is a gift from God to be used wisely.

Biblical Basis: Ephesians 5:16, 17.

Materials Needed: A copy of the Teach 'Toon for each student; pens or pencils; scratch paper; Bibles.

Before Class: Photocopy the Teach 'Toon. See Step 2 for necessary preparation.

Step 1: Have the students poll each other regarding how they would answer the following question: If you learned you were going to die in a couple of years, what difference would it make in the way you spend your time now?

Discuss the students' responses. Say something like, **Even though we don't know when we will die, we all have today to live life to its fullest. Let's think about how to wisely use the gift of time.**

Step 2: Assemble your students into groups of three or four. Each group should look up Ephesians 5:16, 17, and create a commercial jingle or a rap song that gives the main ideas of the text. Be prepared to give your students an example of what you would like for them to do and perhaps some ideas for a tune. Allow willing groups to perform their songs.

Step 3: Give a copy of the Teach 'Toon to each student. Tell everyone to study the drawings and to evaluate the use of time in each situation. Remind your learners that some of the situations can have more than one answer. Don't let students get too conditional or technical in their evaluations. For example, reading a book would generally be considered a good use of time, but it could be argued that reading a bad book is a waste of time.

After evaluating the Teach 'Toon, ask the students to discuss their ideas about the various activities illustrated and their opinions as to the value of each. Be prepared for some distinct differences of opinion.

Discuss the ways your students tend to spend most of their time.

Step 4: Have each person privately complete the following statement on a piece of scratch paper: I would be wise to spend more of my time_____ and less of my time _____.

Close in prayer.

MEDAL OF HONOR

LOOK UP I TIMOTHY 3:1-7 AND TITUS 1:6-9. WHAT DO THEY TELL ABOUT THE QUALIFICATIONS NEEDED FOR A LEADER? THINK ABOUT A LEADER IN YOUR CHURCH. WHAT MAKES HIM OR HER SPECIAL?

— EXAMPLE —

LONG HOURS AWARD
FOR LONG UNTIRING SERVICE
TO OUR CHURCH FAMILY

IN THESE SPACES CREATE "MEDALS OF HONOR" THAT MIGHT BE AWARDED TO PEOPLE IN YOUR CHURCH.

MINISTERING TO THE MINISTER

Main Focus: It is important to show appreciation to our spiritual leaders.

Biblical Basis: 1 Timothy 3:1-7; Titus 1:6-9.

Materials Needed: A copy of the Teach 'Toon for each student; pens or pencils; scratch paper; Bibles; small rewards for Step 1. See **Before Class** regarding a "trivia test." OPTIONAL: A dictionary for Step 2.

Before Class: Photocopy the Teach 'Toon. (This Teach 'Toon can be copied on label paper with an adhesive backing. The completed medals can be drawn with black pen, colored, cut out, and actually awarded to the leader. This type of paper can usually be found in stationery and art supply stores. It's made by Avery and similar companies.)

Gather information about at least one of the leaders, ministers, or youth workers who work in your youth group or church. Think up your own trivia test based on this information. Try questions like, Where were they born? What are their middle names? What are the names of spouses and kids? What sports teams do they root for? What colleges did they attend? What colors do they look best in? What are their duties at church?

Step 1: Give your students the trivia test. (If any of your students are related to the test subjects, let them take the test, but do not let them share answers.) Tell your group the answers and give small rewards for those who gave the most correct responses.

Discuss how tough and demanding a job in spiritual leadership is.

Step 2: Distribute a copy of the Teach 'Toon to every learner. Ask everyone to read the verses that describe what a leader in the church should be. Your students will find that the office of overseer, shepherd, or elder is one that requires responsibility and spiritual maturity. Scripture demands that a minister be temperate (regulated in behavior), above reproach, self-controlled, gentle, respectable, and have a good reputation with outsiders. You may wish to have a dictionary handy to help give clarity.

After your students have read the requirements of a spiritual leader, pass out paper and ask them to create a want ad that might be taken out by a church in need of leadership. Make sure your students note the important qualifications.

Step 3: Tell your students to consider the spiritual leaders in your church or group. Have them work on the Teach 'Toon to create medals that might be awarded for service to the church. Instruct everyone to consider any qualities that would be worthy of a medal.

Step 4: Help your students find a way to say thank you to your leaders for what they have done for the youth. This could involve an awards ceremony where your kids hand out the "Medals of Honor" they have created, an appreciation dinner, a special gift, a letter, or some other means.

Close in a prayer of thanks for your leaders.

— WHAT DID HE SAY? —

MATCH THE CARTOON WITH THE SAYING OF JESUS. OPPOSITE THE DRAWING, WRITE WHAT YOU THINK HE MEANT.

JOHN
3:3-8

LUKE
13:30

MATTHEW
5:29

MATTHEW
8:19-22

LUKE
7:35

MATTHEW
4:18

MARK
10:24,25

SAY WHAT?

Main Focus: To a young person, the teachings of Christ are often deep and obscure. Here are some explanations.

Biblical Basis: Matthew 4:19, 5:29, 8:19-22, 11:19; Mark 10:24, 25; Luke 7:35, 13:30; John 3:3-8.

Materials Needed: Bibles; paper; pens or pencils; a copy of the Teach Toon for each student.

Before Class: Photocopy the Teach Toon. Arrange for a number of people in your church to serve as "mini scholars" to help answer questions written by kids in the group about Gospel passages they don't understand. These people should be prepared to answer the queries and respond personally by mail.

Step 1: Ask your group to complete the following expressions:

Colder than a _____.

Bigger than a _____.

So bad it _____.

Faster than a _____.

Use as many adjectives as you can to complete the expressions. Point out to your students how some of the expressions we use are silly, even nonsensical, while others are merely exaggerations. For example, no one really is faster than lightning, yet we use the expression. Point out that Jesus often used expressions or colorful figures of speech to get his ideas across.

Step 2: Distribute a copy of the Teach Toon to each person. Ask the students to match the drawing with the correct verse, then explain what they think Jesus meant by each statement or expression.

"You must be born again." A person needs a spiritual birth as well as a physical one. This rebirth comes by believing in Christ as Lord (John 3:3-8).

"The first shall be last." Those who seek to exalt themselves will be humbled, and those who serve others will be exalted (Luke 13:30).

"If your eye offends you, pluck it out." Don't let anything stand in the way of obeying God (Matthew 5:29).

"Wisdom is proved right by all her children." A life wisely lived has positive results to show for it (Luke 7:35).

"Let the dead bury their own dead." Don't let any obligation divert you from following Christ (Matthew 8:19-22).

"It is easier for a camel to go through the eye of a needle than for a rich man to enter the kingdom of God." God cannot be God in a person's life if he or she puts anything, especially material gain, in first place of importance (Mark 10:24, 25).

"I will make you fishers of men." Jesus wants to use us to draw people into the kingdom of God (Matthew 4:19).

Step 3: Have your group discover more of the tough or interesting sayings of Jesus by reading one chapter of the Gospels (Luke 6 is a good one for this). Have the kids note on a separate piece of paper all the sayings that are not clear to them, along with their names and addresses. Collect the papers.

Step 4: After class give the papers to the "scholars" who have volunteered to clear up the questions. Make sure they respond to each student's paper within the week.

Close in prayer.

GOOFY GROWTH

CUT OUT THE OBJECTS BELOW AND PASTE THEM WHERE THEY **DON'T** ACTUALLY BELONG.

WHEN YOU'RE DONE
CHECK OUT THIS VERSE:
1 CORINTHIANS 13:11

GROWING IN THE SPIRITUAL WORLD

Main Focus: All Christians should be moving up through the stages of spiritual development.

Biblical Basis: John 3:3-8; 1 Corinthians 3:1, 2; 13:11-13; Ephesians 4:14, 15; Hebrews 5:12-14, 6:1; 1 Peter 2:2.

Materials Needed: Baby pictures of kids in your group; prizes for your contest winners; scissors; glue or rubber cement; Bibles; rolls of butcher paper as described in Step 3; felt pens; paper; pens or pencils; a copy of the Teach 'Toon for every two or three learners.

Before Class: A week or so before class, start collecting baby pictures from parents of your students. Don't let the kids know what you are doing. Photocopy the Teach 'Toon.

Step 1: Carefully display the baby pictures around the room. Place a number near each photo. As the students enter your room, give them pencils and paper and have them try to match the baby pictures with the students. After a few minutes, have your group sit down, then reveal the identity of each baby. Give prizes to the students who get the most correct.

Say something like, **We can see that many of you have grown into people considerably different than when you started. The same is true in the spiritual realm. Christians grow and mature in their Christianity. Let's explore the different stages of growth as a Christian.**

Step 2: Assemble groups of two or three students. Hand out copies of the Teach 'Toon, scissors, glue sticks or rubber cement, and Bibles. Have the students cut off the bottom half of the Teach 'Toon. Then have them cut out items to glue to each picture, matching items that are *inappropriate* for the maturity level of either the baby or the adult. For example, a student might cut out the baby bottle to put in the adult's hand or the newspaper to put in the baby's hand.

When your students have finished, post their lampoons around the room. Read the passages on the Teach 'Toon and ask your students to point out the similarities between what they have created and the people Paul wrote about.

Step 3: Direct the groups to the Scriptures in the **Biblical Basis** section. After they read the passages, each group is to create a growth chart that shows the spiritual journey of a growing Christian. Give a long roll of butcher paper and felt pens to each group. Post their work around the room.

Example:

Step 4: Point out that it is not a bad thing to be a baby Christian, but we want to grow in maturity. Ask your students to work individually to create a formula that would help them to grow spiritually. For example, a learner might write "Spend more time reading the Bible" or "Hang out with Christians who are good influences." Allow the kids who would like to display their work to do so.

Close in prayer.

WHAT DO YOU DO?

YOU'RE IN A HURRY TO MEET WITH A FILM DIRECTOR WHO IS CONSIDERING YOU FOR A ROLE IN A NEW MOVIE. THIS IS A GOLDEN OPPORTUNITY AND YOU CAN'T BE LATE. ON YOUR WAY TO THE MEETING AN ACCIDENT TAKES PLACE RIGHT IN FRONT OF YOU. YOU'RE ABLE TO SWERVE AROUND THE WRECK. THERE IS NO ONE ELSE IN SIGHT.

MELVIN, THE NEW KID AT SCHOOL, IS SHOPPING FOR SCHOOL CLOTHES. HE PULLS A WAD OF MONEY FROM HIS POCKET TO PAY FOR HIS STUFF AND A $20 BILL FLOATS OUT OF THE PILE AND SLIDES UNDER A RACK OF CLOTHES. NOBODY ELSE BUT YOU SEES WHAT HAPPENED.

EVERY DAY, YOUR SCHOOL BUS STOPS IN FRONT OF A HOUSING PROJECT AND PICKS UP A BUNCH OF RAGGED KIDS. ONE DAY YOU ACCIDENTALLY LEAVE YOUR JACKET ON THE BUS. THE NEXT DAY, YOU SEE ONE OF THE KIDS FROM THE PROJECT GETTING ON THE BUS WEARING YOUR JACKET.

A POOR LITTLE OLD LADY IS HAVING A GARAGE SALE. SHE IS A WIDOW AND HER ONLY SON HAS RECENTLY DIED. SHE IS SELLING OFF WHAT SHE CAN TO SURVIVE. YOU'VE JUST DISCOVERED AN EXTREMELY VALUABLE SET OF OLD SPORTS CARDS IN THE DIME BARREL. OBVIOUSLY THE OLD LADY HAS NO IDEA OF WHAT THEY ARE WORTH.

ACTIVE FAITH

Main Focus: Faith to be faith must be put into action.

Biblical Basis: Luke 10:25-37.

Materials Needed: A copy of the Teach Toon for every four or five students; Bibles; blank paper; pencils or pens.

Before Class: Photocopy the Teach Toon.

Step 1: Tell your students, **You have fallen into an ice-filled river. Which person from the following list would you choose to have on the bridge above you: a kid you punched out yesterday, a terrorist, a true believer in Christ, a Hare Krishna, or a famous actress?**

Allow your kids to select whichever person they each prefer. Ask, **Why did you select the person you did? Does being a believer in Christ make a difference in a person's behavior? If not, should it? Why or why not?**

Tell the group you are going to look at some more situations to figure out what to do in each one.

Step 2: Have your students form groups of four or five. Assign each group at least one of the Teach Toon situations to discuss.

Allow a few minutes for each group to talk over its assignment, but do not lead a class discussion at this time.

Step 3: Read aloud or have your students read the parable of the Good Samaritan. Ask questions like, **What do you think of the priest and the Levite who passed on by the wounded man? What do you think their excuses would be for not doing good? What excuses could the Samaritan have come up with for moving along rather than helping?**

Ask the class members to review their responses to the Teach Toon in light of what they have just read. Allow a moment for them to change their responses if they so desire.

Have your learners give you a few examples from school where to do nothing would be to do wrong. Follow it up with examples from home, church, the neighborhood, and even the nation.

Step 4: Invite your students to create a slogan or a motto that could serve as a reminder the next time they run into a situation where to do nothing would be to do wrong. Display their slogans on the walls of your classroom.

Close in prayer.

YOU DRESS 'EM

RUDY AND MAYBEL DON'T HAVE A CLUE ABOUT WHAT IS MODEST OR IMMODEST FOR ANY GIVEN OCCASION. HELP THEM GET THE PICTURE BY DRAWING THE <u>WRONG</u> THING FOR THEM TO WEAR AT THE VARIOUS OCCASIONS BELOW. FOR BEST RESULTS, USE A FELT TIP PEN.

AUNT B'S FUNERAL

THE BEACH

SNOW CAMP

AT GRADUATION

SHOPPING FOR GROCERIES

AT A WEDDING

AT CHURCH

WHERE DO WE DRAW THE LINE?

Main Focus: Although times have changed since biblical days, Christians must still show wisdom in selecting appropriate clothing and behavior.

Biblical Basis: 1 Timothy 2:9, 10.

Materials Needed: A copy of the Teach 'Toon for each student; dark pens or felt pens; paper; Bibles.

Before Class: Photocopy the Teach 'Toon.

Step 1: Read the following situation to your class or write it on the chalkboard: The youth group is planning a mission work trip to a very warm country. You learn that people there feel it is not modest to wear shorts. Do you pack them anyway? Why or why not?

Be prepared for a lively discussion about this issue. Rather than make judgments at this point, stimulate discussion by asking the following questions: **Would it make a difference to you if people in this country thought makeup was immodest? How much would you change to go on this trip?**

Step 2: Ask your students to read 1 Timothy 2:9, 10, and answer the questions below.

1. Does the Bible teach Christians to be modest? (Yes.)

2. Does the Bible define *modesty*? (Sort of—it instructs decency and propriety.)

3. Does the Bible give an example of immodesty? (Yes—braided hair, gold, pearls, and high-priced clothes.)

4. Is braided hair considered immodest today? (If anything, it is considered a modest hairstyle.)

Note that while Paul gave examples of modesty for the times he lived in, we feel sure he would give a few different examples if he were writing to our culture today.

Step 3: Hand out a Teach 'Toon and a pen to each student. Ask the students to dress the characters up in clothing that would be wrong for the occasion. Discuss why it would be inappropriate to wear what they've drawn.

Help your students see that modesty is usually defined by what is appropriate for the situation and culture.

Step 4: Invite your students to create an acrostic out of the word *clothes* that will guide them in principles of wise dressing and living. Let them show their results.

Example:

CHEAP

SIMP**L**E

G**O**DLY

THINK

RIG**H**T

EXAMPLE

STYLE

Close the lesson in prayer.

TATTOO ARTIST *

* WASHABLE, OF COURSE

READ ACTS 27:1-44 AND CREATE TATTOOS SAILORS MIGHT HAVE HAD PUT ON AFTER THEIR VOYAGE WITH PAUL... ESPECIALLY IF THEY LISTENED TO WHAT HE SAID.

CALM IN THE STORM

Main Focus: God uses all kinds of circumstances to show his power.

Biblical Basis: Acts 27:1-44.

Materials Needed: A copy of the Teach 'Toon for each student; pens or pencils; scratch paper; Bibles.

Before Class: Photocopy the Teach 'Toon.

Step 1: Ask your students to relay their experiences sailing the open sea. Did they get seasick? Did they see whales, sharks, or any other creatures? Did they ever go so far out that they could not see land? If so, did they think about what they would do if the ship went down?

Move on to the lesson by saying, **Today we are going to look at a scary but exciting sea adventure that happened to one of the first missionaries of Christianity.**

Step 2: Gather your students into groups of three or four. Assign each group a portion of Acts 27:1-44 to read. Tell them to imagine that they are Luke (who wrote this account in Acts) trying to let the rest of the church know what was happening on this trip, but fearing it might end in disaster.

Have one group write a brief account of the situation in a note to be stuck in a bottle. Another group can write a telegram or a Mayday message that might have been sent by Luke to the church, had such things existed. Ask a group to write a page from Luke's journal or from the captain's log. Have still another group write a last will and testament that might have been written by Paul or one of the sailors.

Share and discuss the results.

Step 3: Distribute a copy of the Teach 'Toon to each student. Explain that the class members are to become tattoo artists. Ask them to put an appropriate design on the arm of one of the shipwrecked sailors who witnessed Paul's actions and believed in Christ as a result. The designs should give the idea of a God who saves people from the worst that can be handed out.

Step 4: Have the students help you create a list of tough problems that young people face. Try to steer the suggestions away from things like car accidents and shipwrecks to things that are more in the kids' world: parents getting a divorce, a best friend moving away, and peer pressure. Write the list on the chalkboard.

Ask your students to suggest ways a person can discover God's power in lousy circumstances. Ask, **What could God teach you through the divorce of your parents or the loss of a good friend? How does God use these situations, even those created by the evil of mankind, to make himself known?**

Invite your class to respond to one of the tough problems listed on the chalkboard. Say, **Think of a person you know who is going through something similar right now. Write down how you can encourage a friend who is facing this problem.**

Discuss the results. Encourage the students to look for an opportunity to share a message of hope this week.

Close in prayer.

ONE FINE DAY AT THE PRUNE-PITTING PLANT

ONCE UPON A TIME, A KIND AND POWERFUL MAN OWNED A PRUNE-PITTING PLANT.

NEEDING TO GO ABROAD FOR BUSINESS, HE PUT HIS COMPANY IN THE HANDS OF HIS WORKMEN...

...WHO PROMPTLY STOPPED WORK AS SOON AS HE LEFT.

THEY RAIDED THE COMPANY SAFE AND TRASHED THE PRUNE-PITTING PLANT

HA, HA, HA!

WHEN IT CAME TIME TO PRODUCE PITTED PRUNES OR SEND PROFITS TO THE OWNER, THEY SAID "FORGET IT!"

SENSING SOMETHING WAS WRONG, THE OWNER HAD HIS COMPANY LAWYER PAY THE PRUNE-PITTING PLANT A VISIT.

UH... HI GUYS!

BUT THE WORKERS BEAT HIM UP AND THREW HIM OUT!

BOOT!!!

THEN THEY PARTIED WITH THE OWNERS' MONEY AS IF THEY HAD NOT A CARE IN THE WORLD.

FINALLY THE OWNER CALLED UP HIS SON AND ASKED HIM TO GO TO THE PLANT TO STRAIGHTEN THINGS OUT.

HEY FELLOWS

THE WORKERS SAID, "THIS GUY WILL BE OUR FUTURE BOSS... AND HE'LL FIRE US!" SO THEY MURDERED HIM.

NOW... YOU END THE STORY!

THE LOUSY TENANTS

Main Focus: Our lives do not belong to us; we are merely God's tenants on this planet.

Biblical Basis: Luke 20:9-19.

Materials Needed: A copy of the Teach 'Toon for every two or three students; pens or pencils; scratch paper; Bibles; a felt pen; a large piece of poster board or butcher paper.

Before Class: Photocopy the Teach 'Toon.

Step 1: Pose the following situation to your class: **Suppose that you wanted to rent a portion of your garage to friends who were going to use it for band practice. What kind of rules and agreements do you think would be fair for your friends, your parents, and any neighbors?** Jot down on a chalkboard any ideas that your students share.

Step 2: Distribute copies of the Teach 'Toon to groups of two or three students. Ask everyone to read the story called "One Fine Day at the Prune-Pitting Plant." They are to write out what they think the ending might be.

When finished, allow the students to share their papers. Read and compare Luke 20:9-19 to the endings the students have created. Are the students' endings similar to the way Jesus ended his parable?

The parable of the wicked tenants is a powerful look at what actually occurred when God's son came to his own people and was rejected and killed. It shows the darkness and the evil that is common among human beings. People today are just as ready to claim ownership of their lives and their souls, not recognizing that God is the true owner of these things.

Step 3: Point out that we are merely tenants in this world and that God wants us to live productive lives that honor him. Tell your students to create a contract that God might write between an owner (God) and a tenant (a young person). The contracts should explain the obligations of the tenant to God. These obligations might include putting effort into harvesting for God (sharing our faith), following the wishes of the owner of our souls (obeying God's Word), or doing our work responsibly to honor our Master.

Have your students show their work when they have completed it.

Step 4: Using a large piece of paper or poster board, take the best of what the students share and create a final version of the contract. Students who are willing may sign it as a promise of their wise occupancy of earth. Post it on the wall after the students have signed it.

Close in prayer.

THE TALE OF THE SENSURROUND HAT

ONCE UPON A TIME, A CRAZY PROFFESSOR INVENTED A VERY STRANGE HAT.

HE CALLED IT "THE SENSURROUND HAT"...

... BECAUSE WHEN YOU PUT IT ON, YOU COULD PROGRAM IT TO SIMULATE ANY KIND OF EXPERIENCE YOU WANTED!

WOW!

FOR EXAMPLE, IN YOUR MIND, YOU COULD BE SKIING IN ASPEN...

...WHILE YOU ACTUALLY ARE SPRAWLED OUT IN BAKERSFIELD.

OOH...AH!

NATURALLY, PEOPLE WERE VERY INTERESTED IN THE SENSURROUND HAT!

ESPECIALLY SINCE IT COULD GIVE YOU ANY SENSATION WITHOUT EFFORT.

SURF HUGE PIPELINE

YOU & 50 PLAYBOY CUTIES

WIN THE WORLD SERIES

BE MISS AMERICA

BEFORE LONG, THE WHOLE NATION HAD "SENSURROUND HATS"... AND VERY LITTLE ELSE WAS GETTING DONE. (BUT NO ONE CARED)

MOMMY, I'M HUNGRY.

LATER KID!

TOTALLY LEGAL, JUST LIKE THE REAL THING, WHAT MORE COULD YOU ASK FOR?

MORE PROGRAMS!

WOULD YOU USE A "SENSURROUND HAT" IF THEY BECAME REAL?

WHAT ARE THE PROBLEMS WITH THIS DEVICE?

WHAT IS IT LIKE THAT WE ALREADY HAVE IN OUR SOCIETY?

DRUGS

Main Focus: We cheat ourselves out of the exciting life God offers us when we go after the fake fun provided by drugs.

Biblical Basis: Ephesians 5:15-18; 1 Thessalonians 5:7, 8.

Materials Needed: Bibles; pens or pencils; scratch paper; a copy of the Teach 'Toon for each learner.

Before Class: Photocopy the Teach 'Toon.

Step 1: On the chalkboard write the following question: Why do kids use drugs or alcohol? Ask the students for their ideas. You will probably get answers such as peer pressure, curiosity, to be cool, for fun, or because of boredom.

Step 2: Distribute a copy of the Teach 'Toon to each student. All the students should read the story, "The Sensurround Hat."

Involve your students in a discussion about the morality of wearing such a hat. Ask questions like, **If there were such a device as a sensurround hat, would you use it? Why or why not? Would it make a difference to you if you *thought* you were experiencing something that you actually were not? Why? Who might a sensurround hat benefit? What are some of the possible dangers from a device like this? In what ways does a hat like this compare to drugs? In what ways might the two differ?**

Step 3: Ask your students to read the passages listed under **Biblical Basis.** Instruct the kids to rewrite in their own words what God says about "substances" and what he desires for people.

Discuss the following ideas: **Do you think God asks us to be filled with the Holy Spirit rather than a substance because he knows this will make us more interesting and dynamic people? Why might it? Although people say they are against drugs because drugs are against the law or because they damage the mind and the body, do you think this is the main spiritual problem with drugs? Would it make a difference if the drug was safe and legal? Would you agree with the statement, "God wants to place his imagination and creativity in us so that we will not want or need artificial fun"?**

Step 4: Distribute scratch paper to the group. Ask your students to create a motto that expresses what God wants to instill into their lives by his presence rather than by chemicals. Share the mottos and post them around the room.

Close in prayer.

PICK A PICTURE AND WRITE A SENTENCE OR TWO THAT DESCRIBES WHAT KIND OF PAIN IS SHOWN. (PAIN IS NOT ALWAYS PHYSICAL... THINK ABOUT IT!)

WRITE A SENTENCE OR TWO

HOW DID A SIMILAR KIND OF PAIN HAPPEN TO JESUS?
JOHN 1:10, 11

LUKE 22:54-61

JOHN 10:20

LUKE 7:30-34

LUKE 22:63-65

LUKE 22:39-46

GOD KNOWS THE PAIN

Main Focus: God knows the pain and loneliness we feel because he felt it himself.

Biblical Basis: Hebrews 13:5, 6.

Materials Needed: A copy of the Teach 'Toon for each student; pens or pencils; scratch paper or card stock; Bibles.

Before Class: Photocopy the Teach 'Toon.

Step 1: Tell your class, **Let's pretend that you must experience pain right now, but you can choose the kind of pain you suffer. You may choose between feeling emotional pain (for example, the loss of a friend) and physical pain (such as from a broken arm).**

Have the students who choose emotional pain go to the right side of the room, while those who choose physical pain go to the left side. No one is allowed to remain in the middle.

Involve your group members in a discussion about why they chose the type of pain they did.

Explain, **During this meeting we are going to be looking at the emotional pain that is common to us all. Jesus knows and has experienced the same pain.**

Step 2: Hand out the Teach 'Toon to your students, and ask them to write a sentence or two explaining what kind of pain is pictured there. If time is short, you may wish to assign selected cartoons to various students. Let the students show and discuss their efforts.

Step 3: Direct attention to the Scripture reference section of the Teach 'Toon. Tell the class members to look up the verses that coincide with the paragraphs they have written and record how Jesus walked a similar path. Have your students share what they have discovered.

Step 4: Read aloud Hebrews 13:5, 6: **"Never will I leave you; never will I forsake you." So we say with confidence, "The Lord is my helper; I will not be afraid. What can man do to me?"**

Pass out scratch paper (or card stock) and pens. Ask your group members to create a motto or a slogan to remember when they are suffering emotional pain. Invite your students to take the mottos home and put them where they can see them when times get tough.

Close in prayer.

~THE SHADOW KNOWS~

DESCRIBE WHAT THE SHADOW KNOWS ABOUT EACH OF THESE PEOPLE.

PART 1

YOU DRAW WHAT THE SHADOW KNOWS.

PART 2

ZACCHAEUS
(SEE LUKE 19:1-10)

ANANIAS (SEE ACTS 5:1-11) SAPPHIRA

SHADOW SELF-PORTRAIT TIME!

PART 3

YOU!

BEING REAL

Main Focus: Being genuine and honest is much better than building a life that is a facade.

Biblical Basis: Acts 5:1-11; Luke 19:1-10.

Materials Needed: Bibles; pencils; a copy of the Teach 'Toon for each student; newsprint; felt pens.

Before Class: Photocopy the Teach 'Toon.

Step 1: Distribute a copy of the Teach 'Toon to each student. Have the kids work on Part 1 of the Teach 'Toon. When they have finished, discuss their observations. Ask, **Do you think it is wrong to wish you were something that you are not? What good things could come from that kind of wish? What are some negative things? Do you think it is wrong to hide the kind of person you really are? Why or why not?**

Step 2: Assemble your students into small groups. Assign one of the two stories from the **Biblical Basis** section to each group. Ask the students to imagine that they are reporters for the *Jerusalem Snoop*, a daily newspaper. Distribute large sheets of paper or newsprint and felt pens to each group. Have the groups create a front page edition covering one of the two Bible stories. Allow time for the groups to share what they have created and post the papers on the wall.

Have your students go back to Part 2 of the Teach 'Toon and finish the shadow drawing that would match Zacchaeus, Ananias, and Sapphira. Involve your students in a discussion by asking the following questions: **What did Ananias and Sapphira do wrong? What did Zacchaeus do right? What kind of facade or false front did Ananias and Sapphira put up? What seems to be the difference in heart desire between Ananias, Sapphira, and Zacchaeus? What alternatives did Ananias and Sapphira have?** (They could have held on to all of their money, they could have given a portion but been honest in what they declared, or they could have given all of their money.) **What do you think was each person's motive for giving? Which kind of person would you want as a friend? Why?**

Step 3: Revisit the Teach 'Toon one more time and ask the students to sketch in silhouettes of what they would like to be inside (Part 3). For example, someone could sketch the outline of a person playing a guitar to symbolize a desire to create music for God's glory. Another student could sketch someone smiling because of the peace and joy deep inside. Discuss what the students have done.

Close in prayer, asking God to transform these desires into reality.

TEMPTING SITUATIONS

FIGHTING TEMPTATION

Main Focus: We must be aware of and avoid temptation.

Biblical Basis: 2 Samuel 11.

Materials Needed: One copy of the Teach 'Toon for each student; Bibles; pencils or pens; index cards. OPTIONAL: Poster paper for Step 2, or you can let the students use the backs of their Teach 'Toons for the news releases.

Before Class: Photocopy the Teach 'Toon. Your class will assemble into small groups to read 2 Samuel 11, one section of the chapter per group. Divide the chapter into enough sections for the number of small groups you plan to have. If your class is small, have the students work individually. TIP: To save class time, write each Scripture portion reference on a card to give to each group.

Step 1: Ask your students to describe incidents when they were at the wrong place at the wrong time. Perhaps a girl student accidentally walked into a boys rest room. Maybe a kid showed up to see a movie that was playing at another theater. What were their feelings when they realized their mistakes? What did they do? Tie this discussion into today's lesson by explaining that you and your students are going to learn about a moment when King David was definitely in the wrong place at the wrong time—the story of David and Bathsheba.

Step 2: Assemble your class into small groups and assign each group a section of 2 Samuel 11 to explore. Make sure each group has a Bible, pens or pencils, and poster paper. Group members are to read their section and create a news release, a newspaper article, or a television news report about what they learn. Have each group read or describe its report to the class. Discuss the following questions:

1. **Where should David have been?** (At the battlefield)

2. **What should he have done when he realized he intruded on Bathsheba's privacy?** (Left)

3. **What should he have done when he learned that Bathsheba was married?** (Left her alone)

Step 3: Distribute a copy of the Teach 'Toon to each class member. Point out that while few of us are likely to see a beautiful person taking a bath on the next door neighbor's roof, temptation to do wrong is something that can happen anytime, anywhere, to anyone.

There are three boxes on the Teach 'Toon labeled school, friends, and home—areas where temptations can arise. Students are to draw examples of the kind of temptations they may face in each situation. Someone might draw a person cheating on a test at school; another could show two friends gossiping about a third. Although the students can work together to think of ideas, each person is to fill out his or her own Teach 'Toon.

As you review the temptations your class has come up with, collect the finished Teach 'Toons and post them on the walls. As an important part of your discussion, ask the students what they could do to avoid or resist their examples of temptation. For instance, cheating in school will not be a temptation at all if a student spends time studying.

Step 4: Students are to work individually and privately to select three temptations that they would find most difficult to resist. Do not ask them to share this information.

Close the session by asking your class to spend a few moments in quiet prayer asking God to give each person the strength and the will to resist temptation.

THE COMPANY YOU KEEP

Main Focus: Bad company corrupts good morals.

Biblical Basis: Proverbs 1:10; 1 Corinthians 5:6-11, 15:33; 2 Thessalonians 3:6.

Materials Needed: One copy of the Teach 'Toon per student; several Bibles; heavy card stock paper; scissors; colored pencils or pens.

Before Class: Photocopy the Teach 'Toon.

Step 1: Ask your students to stand on the right side of the room if they agree with the following statement or to stand on the left side if they disagree: "Generally, a person becomes like the people he or she hangs out with."

After the students have picked their side of the room, ask several kids to explain why they made the choices they did. After discussing the pros and cons of the statement, allow any who wish to do so to change sides.

Step 2: Have volunteers read the Scripture passages listed above. Jot on the chalkboard any important points regarding the keeping of bad company. Have your students work in twos or threes to rewrite 1 Corinthians 15:33 like a children's rhyme or, if they prefer, a rap song.

Step 3: Distribute copies of the Teach 'Toon. Ask the class members to decide what they would do if two friends ripped off Sam's Market. Discuss the following questions:

1. **The kid in the middle is obviously concerned. What options are pictured, suggested, or available to him?** (The police are nearby, there's a phone, Mel's Coffee Hut is a good place to talk things out, and Sam is available.)

2. **What could happen to the kid in the center if his friends are caught?**

3. **What advice would you give to the center kid? What should he say to his friends?**

Step 4: Have the students create wallet-size cards to serve as reminders of the need to select companions wisely. Provide card stock, scissors, and colored pens or pencils. Each student is to design a card featuring the theme or the main point of what he or she has learned. Have each kid place the card in a wallet or a purse next to any photos of friends.

Close in prayer.

WHAT IS THE BIGGEST THING KIDS YOUR AGE WORRY ABOUT?

DRAW IT HERE...

WORRY

Main Focus: Kids have real things to worry about; God gives real reasons not to.

Biblical Basis: Matthew 6:25-34; Philippians 4:6, 7.

Materials Needed: One copy of the Teach 'Toon for each student; extra paper (or the back of the Teach 'Toon copies); markers; pencils; Bibles.

Before Class: Photocopy the Teach 'Toon.

Step 1: Allow the students individually or in pairs to complete the Teach 'Toon. Have several volunteers tell what they drew, or collect all the Teach 'Toons and show them to the class. Discuss the nature of each worry and why it is a worry to young people. Ask, **Do a lot of people worry about this? Do you think it's a real problem or something not likely to be a threat? What would happen if this problem really occurred?**

Pick the top three or four worries and save them for later use.

Step 2: Have volunteers read sections of Matthew 6:25-34 aloud. Assemble the students into pairs or threes. Their assignment is to list all the "anti-worry" principles they can find in the passage. Have them decide on a favorite and be ready to explain it.

As you and the class discuss the results, be sure to point out the following principles: God, who gave us life, values us and will take care of the details of life (verse 25); God takes care of even the lowliest creatures he created—he'll take care of us (verse 26); worrying is not helpful (verse 27); God's care is better than even the richest man's care of himself (verses 28-30); a worried Christian is like a pagan—without faith in God (verses 30-32); God wants us to pursue his kingdom and righteousness—worry gets in the way (verse 33); living one day at a time helps defeat worry (verse 34). Jot these ideas on the chalkboard.

Step 3: Return to the three or four Teach 'Toons you set aside, and ask the students to describe how the various principles relate to each worry. For example, a person worried about dating can rest assured that God cares and is personally involved in a Christian's relationships. A Christian who is pursuing righteousness won't have to worry about going too far on a date.

Read Philippians 4:6, 7 aloud. Ask the students to describe what they might specifically pray for if they are worried about some of the problems discussed.

Step 4: Give everyone a blank sheet of paper (or use the back of the Teach 'Toon). Say, **I want you to work individually to create a contract between you and God. In your contract, describe what your biggest worry in life is, then tell God that you commit it to his care. Write down your favorite passage that we studied today; you can write it in your own words. Sign and date your contract and take it with you.**

Close in silent prayer, giving students a chance to commit their worries to God.

HELPING OUT THE YOUTH GROUP

Main Focus: Help your kids identify ways they can serve in the youth group.

Biblical Basis: Proverbs 11:24, 25; 21:13; Matthew 25:14-30.

Materials Needed: A copy of the Teach 'Toon for every three or four students; pens or pencils; scratch paper or index cards; Bibles. OPTIONAL: Various magazines for Step 1.

Before Class: Photocopy the Teach 'Toon. Step 5 requires you to prepare a list in your mind of various areas of need in your youth group that kids in your class could fill. You might need someone to help set up the classroom before each meeting. Perhaps you'd like a student to read the announcements. Several students could each take a short phone list to pass on vital youth group news. Think of as many service areas as you can.

Step 1: OPTIONAL: To get the students thinking about serving others, have them work in groups of three or four to look through magazines for examples of things people could use to serve others: an ad for a car—someone could drive people to church in a car, an ad for food—someone could collect food for the hungry, or a picture of money—money can be used many ways in service to others. Encourage your learners to use their imaginations. Students can tear the examples out. Discuss what they find.

Step 2: Have the same groups work on the Teach 'Toon assignment. Talk about the results, suggesting areas of service the kids may not have thought about.

Step 3: Read Matthew 25:14-30 aloud. (It's rather long; you may prefer to simply tell the story in your own words.) Read or have volunteers read Proverbs 11:24, 25 and 21:13. Discuss the specific points these passages make about service.

Step 4: Distribute index cards or scratch paper, one to each student. Ask the students to work privately to list at least one talent or ability they possess—anything that could be of possible service to the Lord. For example, if some kids possess athletic ability, tell them to think of some way God might use an athlete in his service. Students are not to sign the cards.

Collect and discuss each card. Create a chart on the chalkboard that lists all the talents your group possesses and the various ways God can use them in his service. Tie these areas of service in with the needs of the youth group. For example, someone with musical ability could lead a song at a youth group event.

Step 5: Discuss in detail the list of youth group needs that you prepared before class. Ask the students to meet the needs they can fill themselves, according to the chart you created. Say, **The cards were anonymous. I know the talents that some of you possess, but not all. It's up to you to tell me if you'd like to volunteer your services for any of the needs we have. Don't worry if you think you might not know exactly how to do something. I'll be glad to help you learn and get into it. Please talk to me after class if you want to be involved.**

Suggest that learners put their initials beside any area on the chart that they are interested in. Close in prayer.

If the response is poor, don't be afraid to "tag" a few kids in the near future. Sometimes kids want to try something new but they don't know how to begin.

TV TIME

FILL IN THE TVS WITH THE NAMES OF SHOWS YOU WATCH. INDICATE WHICH ONES YOU WATCH A LOT AND WHICH ONES YOU VIEW NOW AND THEN. IF YOU DON'T WATCH TV AT HOME, MAYBE YOU SEE IT IN SCHOOL OR AT FRIENDS' HOMES. YOU CAN PUT THE TITLES OF FAVORITE VIDEOS IN, TOO.

NOW FIGURE OUT HOW MUCH TIME IT TAKES TO WATCH EACH SHOW. ADD UP ALL THE TIMES TO GET AN APPROXIMATE IDEA OF HOW MUCH TIME YOU WATCH TELEVISION EACH WEEK:

TIME:

TELEVISION

Main Focus: Is television an accurate representation of our society? Do we watch too much of it? Do we think critically about what we see?

Biblical Basis: Luke 9:59-62.

Materials Needed: A copy of the Teach 'Toon for every learner; pens or pencils; scratch paper; Bibles; a copy of the *TV Guide* for every three or four students; a list of prepared Bible questions (see **Before Class**).

Before Class: Photocopy the Teach 'Toon. Prepare about a dozen Bible trivia questions tailored to your students' level—not too hard, not too easy. Suggestions are as follows:

> Who named all the living creatures? (Adam—Genesis 2:19, 20)
> Who was Samson's girlfriend? (Delilah—Judges 16:3, 4)
> Who was the missing 12-year old found in the temple? (Jesus—Luke 2:42-46)
> Who lost his head for criticizing King Herod? (John the Baptist—Matthew 14:1-10)
> Who denied Jesus three times? (Peter—Luke 22:54-62)
> What's another name for Jacob? (Israel—Genesis 35:10)
> Who clobbered Goliath? (David—1 Samuel 17:4, 50)

Step 1: Hand out the *TV Guides* and pens or pencils to small groups of three or four students. Have each group find and work the crossword puzzle. (If you like, you can work the crossword with the entire class; just read the clues and allow volunteers to suggest the answers.)

When the kids are done, see how they did. It's not necessary to go over all the answers; just ask the group members to give an approximate percentage of the answers they knew.

Now ask your students to answer your prepared Bible questions. Allow only one answer per student to prevent Bible hotshots from dominating the discussion. Count off how many the students got right. Compare their knowledge of TV trivia with their knowledge of the Bible. Television is probably the hands-down winner. Point this out and say, **Television probably has a greater influence on us than the Bible has.**

Step 2: Now ask the groups to look through the *TV Guides* for program advertisements. Students should write a list of the sort of things these ads promote as reasons to watch: sexual situations, violence, tragedy, uplifting stories, Christian principles (a Billy Graham special or the like)—anything they can find.

Allow several minutes for the students to work. Discuss what they found and jot notes on the chalkboard. Ask, **How many of the TV shows tried to appeal to our baser instincts? How many shows sounded stupid? What were the ones you'd like to see? Why did they interest you?**

Step 3: Let everyone work individually on the Teach Toon. Discuss the amount of time students spend watching the tube. Do they think it's too much? Too little? How does it compare with the amount of time spent talking to mom and dad, talking to God, attending youth group events, and so forth?

Have your class carefully consider the type of influence the worst of the TV programs have on kids compared to the influence the Bible has. Which has the most positive influence? Which is the better guide for living?

Step 4: Say, **One of the chief problems with television is that it can distract us from more important things. Many kids your age would rather be outside playing than sitting in front of the tube—but then again, many would rather waste time watching TV than studying for a test! TV can be an excuse to ignore important chores. The worst thing is when it takes time away from God. Don't answer this out loud, but how many of you ever missed church to watch a televised football game or skipped a youth meeting to catch a show?**

Read Luke 9:59-62. Ask the students to describe the distractions that people used as excuses to ignore Christ. (NOTE: In the case of the man who wanted to bury his father, many Bible scholars believe the father was probably not dead, just old. What an excuse!) Have them tell what someone might have said if TV was big back then.

Step 5: Have each group create "Agent Xork's Report to the Galactic Council," which describes an alien's perception of our planet as if all he knew was what he saw on your students' favorite shows. Would he think that all little children are great with one-liners? Are all parents handsome and understanding? Are all cities constantly full of shootings, car chases, and robbers? Are all problems solved by force or violence? In other words, is TV an accurate reflection of real life?

Listen to each group's report, then encourage your students to examine the wisdom of protracted television watching. Do they think about what they watch with a critical eye, or do they just drink it in? Do they think all problems are resolved in half an hour, or do they understand that real life is more complicated than that?

Close in prayer.

SELF-ESTEEM

Main Focus: Let's take a look at the things that make us important in God's eyes in contrast to the things that make us important in the world's eyes.

Biblical Basis: 1 Samuel 16:7; Galatians 5:22, 23.

Materials Needed: One copy of the Teach 'Toon for each student; pencils or pens; Bibles; markers; heavy card stock paper for Step 4. Step 3 calls for small boxes that students can draw and write on. Cereal boxes (even the single-serving kind) or shoe boxes that have been covered with white paper are fine. You'll need one box for every three or four students. The first step calls for a few dollar bills, a give-away Bible, a soda and a candy bar, or some other reward.

Before Class: Photocopy the Teach 'Toon and prepare the boxes as described above. Hide a few dollars in a Bible that you can give away.

Step 1: When ready to begin, place the soda, the candy bar, and the Bible with the hidden money where everyone can see them. Say, **I'm always telling you that the Bible is a valuable book. Who can give me some reasons why it's worth so much?** Allow several students to respond, then ask for a volunteer to come forward. Ask the student to pick one of the items he or she would like to have and explain why.

If the volunteer picks either the soda or the candy, give them both to the student, then reveal the money inside the Bible. You keep the money and the Bible and say, **There's more value here than meets the eye!**

If the volunteer picks the Bible, give him or her the money and all the items (with great fanfare). Explain, **One of the reasons the Bible contains so much of value is that it tells us how we can become valuable people! If you want to feel like you are a valuable, worthwhile person, pay close attention to today's lesson.**

Step 2: Distribute the Teach 'Toon copies, one per student. Say, **Look at the things surrounding the kid in the middle. Underline all the things that our society strongly believes makes a person important. For example, being rich makes a person important in most people's eyes. When you've done that, circle all the things that God probably values in our lives.**

Discuss the students' responses. Read 1 Samuel 16:7, and discuss how it relates to what the kids have learned from the Teach 'Toon exercise.

Step 3: Distribute the boxes and markers to groups of three or four students. Explain that Galatians 5:22, 23 lists many of the things that God values in a person. Have the students study the passage and write the nine important words as a list of ingredients on the front of their boxes. Students can dream up nice titles for their boxes, such as "Instant Importance!" or "How to Become Valuable!"

Display the boxes, then discuss and sum up what the students have learned. Have the class spend some time thinking of ways God might use a kid who really has any of these good things. Be sure to point out the good news that all nine things are just some of the great gifts from God, available to anyone who wants to walk with him.

Step 4: Give each student materials to make a simple certificate that features his or her favorite characteristic from Galatians. The student writes the characteristic (love, joy, peace, and so on) and one action he or she could perform that would demonstrate the characteristic to a friend or a family member. For example, someone might write, "Patience. I promise to patiently baby-sit my little sister one night this week so my folks can go out for dinner." The certificate is then given to the appropriate person during the week.

Close in prayer and encourage the kids to try out their certificates.

TRASH CANS & MEDALS

CHECK OUT THE SITUATIONS BELOW. JUDGE HOW GOOD OR BAD EACH ACTION IS. IF IT'S GOOD, GIVE IT ONE OR MORE "MEDALS OF HONOR." IF IT'S BAD, GIVE IT ONE OR MORE "TRASH CANS." YOU CAN DRAW THE MEDALS AND TRASH CANS, OR YOU CAN JUST WRITE PLUSES (+) OR MINUSES (−) NEXT TO EACH PANEL.

Walking in the Light

Main Focus: Your students can choose to walk in God's light or in Satan's darkness; there is no middle ground or neutral territory.

Biblical Basis: Isaiah 64:6; Luke 11:23; John 3:19-21, 8:12; Romans 3:23; Ephesians 2:10, 5:8, 9; Hebrews 11:6.

Materials Needed: A copy of the Teach 'Toon for every two or three students; pens or pencils; scratch paper; Bibles. Your meeting room needs lights that can be switched on and off (see Step 1); otherwise, provide a bright flashlight. OPTIONAL: Step 4 requires your students to draw light bulbs. If you like, provide sheets of bright yellow paper.

Before Class: Photocopy the Teach 'Toon.

Step 1: Flip the room lights on and off several times (use a flashlight if there are no lights). Say, **Notice that the lights are either on or off. There is no middle ground. I suppose we could filter the light or partially block it off, but in reality the lights are on or off. Everywhere in the universe there is either the presence of light or the absence of light—there is nothing in between. In the same way, a person either walks in God's light or walks in Satan's darkness; there is no other alternative. You either live for God or you live for Satan. The Bible makes it clear that there is no middle ground or neutral territory.**

Step 2: Gather your students into groups of two or three. Give each group a copy of the Teach 'Toon and a pen or a pencil. Explain, **I want you to pretend that you are like movie critics who award thumbs up or thumbs down to movies they view. Look at the various cartoons on your Teach 'Toon. If a cartoon depicts something really bad, award it four trash cans. If it's not so bad, give it one, two, or three trash cans. If it's good, award it one to four medals of honor. You can write the number of trash cans and medals or you can draw little symbols.**

Notice that each cartoon has a calendar indicating the chronology of events. According to the Bible, *all our righteous acts are like filthy rags* (Isaiah 64:6), *all have sinned and fall short of the glory of God* (Romans 3:23), and *without faith it is impossible to please God* (Hebrews 11:6). These passages and many others reveal that no good works we do before we are saved by Christ mean anything at all to God. They are still deeds done in darkness (see John 3:19-21). But after we become Christians, our good works are pleasing to the Lord. We have been *created in Christ Jesus to do good works, which God prepared in advance for us to do* (Ephesians 2:10). Therefore, even the good things in the cartoons should receive four trash cans if they come before conversion.

Point all of this out to your students *after* they display their completed Teach 'Toons. Say, **From God's point of view, if we haven't come to know him as our Lord and Savior, all our best deeds are worthless. Only when we become Christians can we start to live in the light!**

You can also mention Luke 11:23: *"He who is not with me is against me, and he who does not gather with me, scatters."*

Step 3: Hand out paper or use the backs of the Teach 'Toon copies. Tell the same groups to read Ephesians 5:8, 9 in their Bibles. In that passage the fruit of the light is said to consist of *all goodness, righteousness and truth.* Have the group members think of several examples of things people their age could do that would be good, righteous, or truthful. (Prompt some groups to think of things at school, other groups to think of things at home, and so forth.) The groups can list examples or draw cartoons of at least one example. Walk from group to group offering suggestions and encouragement.

After a few minutes, discuss what the kids have come up with.

Step 4: Jesus said, *"I am the light of the world. Whoever follows me will never walk in darkness, but will have the light of life"* (John 8:12). Give each student a few minutes to draw a large light bulb with John 8:12 (or a slogan based on it) written on the bulb. Display the drawings on the wall for the next few meetings.

Before you close in prayer, explain the steps a person must take to be saved. Offer your time to anyone who would like to talk after class.

WHERE'S WEIRDO?

FIND THE WEIRD-LOOKING KID IN THE CROWD BELOW. THEN, FIND AND CIRCLE HIS STUPID-LOOKING CAT, THE SILLY SUPER-HERO LUNCH PAIL HE DROPPED, HIS CAP WITH THE PROPELLOR AND HIS AUTOGRAPHED PICTURE OF KERMIT THE FROG.

HI! I'M WEIRDO. SEE IF YOU CAN FIND ME BELOW...

CARING FOR THE SOCIAL OUTCAST

Main Focus: Jesus accepted and loved even the "social outcasts"— so should we.

Biblical Basis: Matthew 5:43-48; Luke 10:25-37.

Materials Needed: A copy of the Teach Toon for every pair of students; pens or pencils; scratch paper; Bibles.

Before Class: Photocopy the Teach Toon.

Step 1: Students should work in pairs to complete the Teach Toon. When finished, discuss the following questions: **What are some things that might make people "social outcasts" at school? What would it take for them to be accepted by other people? How do you think Christ would want us to treat them?**

Step 2: Assemble the students into groups of four or five. On the left side of the chalkboard list the following four situations: barfed in class, zipper open during speech, hurt falling down school stairs, love note discovered. Along the top of the board, write "Most Popular Kid" and "School Jerk."

Assign one situation to each group (double up if necessary). Each group is to create a short skit that describes the likely reaction of classmates to the situation. For example, what would people in school say to his face if the most popular student barfed in class? What would they say to and about the school jerk who barfed? Each member of the group should play a role in the skit. One can be the popular kid, one the school jerk, and the rest can be classmates.

Have the groups present their skits, discussing each in turn. Probe your students' sense of right and wrong, justice and injustice. Why is a popular person treated differently than a jerk? Is it fair or unfair? How should a Christian behave? If a Christian treats the school jerk like a real human being, what will people think of the Christian?

Step 3: Read Luke 10:25-37 (or have volunteers read sections). Ask your students, **What did the priest and the Levite do? What did the Samaritan do? If you had the same sort of attitude as the priest and the Levite, how would you treat a school jerk who barfed on the desk next to yours, got caught with his zipper down, fell down the stairs, or wrote a love note that everyone saw? What if you had the Samaritan's attitude?**

Brainstorm some real, practical things a person could do or say to help out a kid in the above situations. If time permits, have the students suggest other situations that happen in school.

Step 4: Let your learners work in pairs to reword Matthew 5:43-48 in light of today's study. Tell them to write it as if Jesus had been talking about "popular" and "dweeb" kids in place of friends, enemies, those who love you, tax collectors, and brothers. Have the students share their verses.

Close in prayer.

Weigh It for Yourself

The Bible passage you've looked at today, 1 Chronicles 28:8-10, gives several principles that—if followed—will help you live a great and meaningful life. Are you following these principles in your life? Let's find out. Read each principle and its paraphrased version. If it's something you usually do, stack it (by drawing a line) on the scale's platform. When finished, count the number of principles and compare that number to the chart below. No one will look at the results except you.

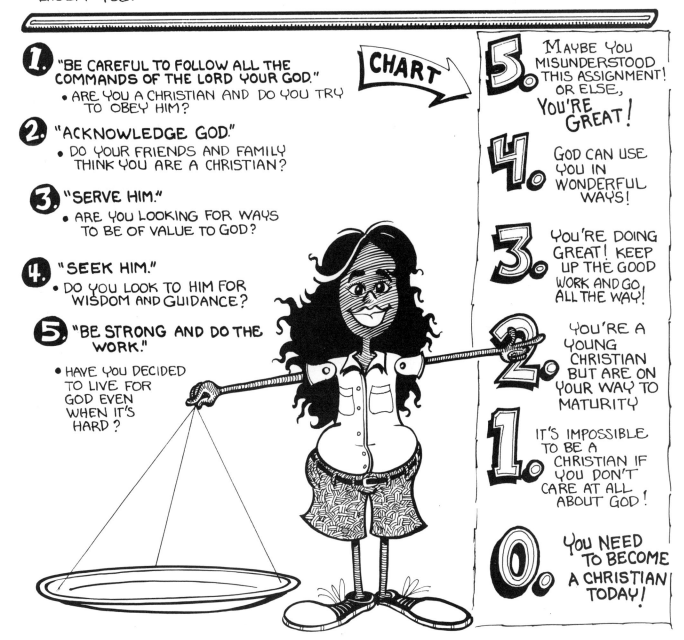

1. "BE CAREFUL TO FOLLOW ALL THE COMMANDS OF THE LORD YOUR GOD."
   • ARE YOU A CHRISTIAN AND DO YOU TRY TO OBEY HIM?

2. "ACKNOWLEDGE GOD."
   • DO YOUR FRIENDS AND FAMILY THINK YOU ARE A CHRISTIAN?

3. "SERVE HIM."
   • ARE YOU LOOKING FOR WAYS TO BE OF VALUE TO GOD?

4. "SEEK HIM."
   • DO YOU LOOK TO HIM FOR WISDOM AND GUIDANCE?

5. "BE STRONG AND DO THE WORK."
   • HAVE YOU DECIDED TO LIVE FOR GOD EVEN WHEN IT'S HARD?

CHART →

5. MAYBE YOU MISUNDERSTOOD THIS ASSIGNMENT! OR ELSE, YOU'RE GREAT!

4. GOD CAN USE YOU IN WONDERFUL WAYS!

3. YOU'RE DOING GREAT! KEEP UP THE GOOD WORK AND GO ALL THE WAY!

2. YOU'RE A YOUNG CHRISTIAN BUT ARE ON YOUR WAY TO MATURITY

1. IT'S IMPOSSIBLE TO BE A CHRISTIAN IF YOU DON'T CARE AT ALL ABOUT GOD!

0. YOU NEED TO BECOME A CHRISTIAN TODAY!

GOD'S RECIPE FOR LIVING

Main Focus: Let God's priorities be your priorities.

Biblical Basis: 1 Chronicles 28:8-10.

Materials Needed: Bibles; pens or pencils; writing paper; markers; large paper for making maps (see Step 4); a copy of the Teach 'Toon for each student.

Before Class: Photocopy the Teach 'Toon.

Step 1: The Bible gives us directions for living. To get your learners to think about the value of knowing and following directions, try this: Ask three or four students to describe how to get from your classroom to their homes. They have to give accurate street names, landmarks, number of blocks, and so on, as if you had no knowledge of the area. You may find that many kids don't even know the street names.

Say, **The Bible gives us directions for living fun, successful lives. But we must learn those directions accurately, and we must follow them closely.**

Step 2: Distribute writing paper and pens or pencils. Have groups of three or four students study 1 Chronicles 28:8-10. Tell the students to find as many "Directions to Live By" as they can. They should be able to find at least five easily. The Teach 'Toon activity in Step 3 will sum up all the principles.

Step 3: Have the students work individually to complete the Teach 'Toon activity.

When finished, discuss each direction (principle of successful Christian living) and go over the promises in 1 Chronicles 28:8-10: The people who obey God will possess the land, God will be found by them, anyone who ignores him will be rejected forever. In discussing these promises, use language that kids can understand. They probably don't care about possessing the land, but they would love to know that God wants to give them fun, exciting lives!

Step 4: To tie in the idea of following God's biblical directions with the specific instructions of the 1 Chronicles passage, have your students work in groups to create "Spiritual Guide Maps." Each map is to feature all of the principles discussed, arranged as landmarks on a road map that someone could follow from the start to "God's Side."

Display the maps on the wall and encourage your learners to follow the maps to fun, godly lives.

Close in prayer.

MIND POLLUTION OR ??

WHICH OF THE THINGS IN THIS PICTURE ARE INDISPUTABLY MIND POLLUTION? WHICH <u>COULD</u> BE AND THEREFORE MUST BE SCREENED, WHICH ARE O.K.? CIRCLE THE POLLUTION, PUT A SQUARE AROUND THE POSSIBLE POLLUTION AND A TRIANGLE AROUND THOSE WHICH ARE O.K.

No Dumping Allowed

Main Focus: We need to be careful to filter pollution out of our minds.

Biblical Basis: Romans 1:20-32; Colossians 3:12-14; 2 Timothy 3:2-5; 2 Peter 1:5-8.

Materials Needed: A copy of the Teach 'Toon for each student; pens or pencils; scratch paper; Bibles.

Before Class: Photocopy the Teach 'Toon.

Step 1: Lead into the subject of things we put into our minds by talking about things we put into our bodies. Ask, **What is the grossest thing you have ever eaten on purpose or accidentally? Would you eat anything for enough money? If you found a well-cooked cockroach in your hamburger, what would you do?**

Point out that most people are repulsed at the idea of eating pollution, even if it might not harm them. Explain that many people seem not nearly as concerned about the junk they allow their minds to feast on.

Step 2: Assemble your class into groups of three or four students. Hand out paper and pencils to each group. Tell the students to write "Christians should take in . . ." on the left side of their papers and "Christians should keep out . . ." on the right side. Ask the students to explore the Scriptures in the **Biblical Basis** section, then list which ideas found in the Bible belong on the right side of the paper and which belong on the left side.

When finished, call on several kids to describe what they have learned.

Step 3: Distribute a Teach 'Toon copy to each person. Ask everyone to decide which of the situations pictured on the page are indisputably mind pollution, which could be mind pollution and so must be monitored, and which are healthy to dwell on. Discuss the results.

Step 4: After your discussion, ask your students to review the Teach 'Toon once again to see if there is an area indicated on the page that they should be more cautious in avoiding or screening. Also ask them to see if there is an area that they should concentrate more of their mental effort upon.

Close in prayerful consideration.

IMPORTANT LINKS

Read each cartoon. On the right, write what positive thing might happen because of what was said in each drawing. On the bottom one, draw something you could say or do that would be an important link in a chain of salvation.

WITNESSING

Main Focus: This lesson makes it a little less difficult to tell a friend about Christ.

Biblical Basis: Luke 5:27-32; Acts 8:26-39.

Materials Needed: A copy of the Teach 'Toon for every two or three students; pens or pencils; scratch paper; Bibles; scissors; tape.

Before Class: Photocopy the Teach 'Toon.

Step 1: To help your students focus their attention on today's subject, tell them about the person who led you to the Lord or who was most instrumental in your Christian life. Explain, **It's people who lead people to Christ. Virtually no one becomes a Christian all by themselves. But what about you? Have you ever told someone how to become a Christian? Many people find it difficult or impossible to open up and talk about a person's need for God and salvation. Today we are going to take a look at some simple tips that will make it a little easier for you to become involved in the process of leading another person to Jesus Christ.**

Step 2: Bring the students together in groups of four or more. Assign Luke 5:27-32 to half the groups and Acts 8:26-39 to the others. Each group is to study its passage and create a radio or a TV news broadcast script describing the passage. The scripts should answer the who, what, where, when, and why questions and should pay particular attention to who did the witnessing and how they did it. In the Luke passage, it's Levi (also known as Matthew) that the students are to focus on. He threw a party to attract his friends and let them see Jesus for themselves. In Acts, Philip talks one-on-one with the Ethiopian. Ask the groups to quickly share their scripts. They can give you the highlights or actually present an imaginary newscast.

Discuss the two different methods used by Levi and Philip. Say, **Raise your hand if you think it would be easier for you to throw a party and let everyone enjoy a good time while you smiled and behaved like an excited Christian, as Levi did. Raise your hand if you think it would be easier for you to tell a friend about your faith privately as Philip did. How many of you would feel uncomfortable either way?**

Point out that there are several reasons why people get nervous at the thought of telling others about Christ: not knowing where to find passages in the Bible, concern over tough questions, fear of rejection, not knowing where to begin, insecurity over one's own Christian walk, and so forth.

Step 3: Tell your students, **What people often don't realize is that leading a person to the Lord is like putting together links to form a chain. Each link represents a step that a non-Christian takes toward the Lord. One link might be something simple, like coming to a fun youth group event. Another link might be hearing a single Bible verse at one of our studies—a verse that sinks in and makes the person think. Another link could be the act of watching a friend become a happy Christian. You see, there are many steps a person takes before he or she actually makes a commitment to Jesus Christ. The important thing is this: You might not be good at presenting the whole Gospel to a friend, but you can forge another link in the chain by inviting your pal to one of our fun events. Anyone can do that. Yet it could be one of the most important links in the chain. God could use another person at that event to draw your friend even closer to salvation.**

Distribute the Teach 'Toon, which features five paper links, four with suggested steps that can draw a person to Christ. The fifth is blank so that your students can think of more steps.

When the assignment is complete, discuss what the students have written and drawn, then use scissors and tape to make a chain out of the links. Hang the chain where your students can view it.

Step 4: Allow the students a few seconds to think privately about a link they could do that would possibly be a part of the chain leading to a friend's salvation. Remind them that God honors them for even the small steps they help a person take.

Close in prayer.

PROBLEM CHILD—

TAKE A LOOK AT THE FOLLOWING SITUATIONS. DECIDE WHAT YOU WOULD SAY OR DO IF **YOU** WERE THE MOM OR DAD. DRAW OR WRITE IT IN THE PROPER PANEL. BE SURE TO EXPLAIN IN DETAIL **WHAT** YOU'D DO AND WHY.

THIS IS THE PRINCIPAL'S OFFICE, MR. FARNSBUSH!

NOT AGAIN...

YOUR DAUGHTER'S GRADES ARE LOUSY. WHAT WOULD YOU SAY AND DO TO HELP HER OUT?

YOUR ROOM IS ALWAYS A DISASTER! I KEEP THE REST OF HOUSE CLEAN AND I EXPECT **YOU** TO KEEP YOUR ROOM CLEAN!

THINK OF SOME GOOD STEPS THAT WILL MOTIVATE JUNIOR TO KEEP HIS ROOM PICKED UP...

THE KIDS ARE SO EXPENSIVE TO CARE FOR. THEY HAVE SO MANY NEEDS— AND SO MANY WANTS! BUT WE JUST DON'T HAVE THE MONEY TO DO EVERYTHING!

WHAT DO WE DO?

WHAT SHOULD YOU DO? WHAT CAN THE KIDS DO?

BURP!

DAD! GIMME A HUNDRED BUCKS! ME AN' DA BOYZ WANNA HAVE A PARTY!

THIS KID IS WELL ON THE WAY TO MAJOR PROBLEMS. WHAT WOULD YOU DO IF YOU WERE HIS DAD?

PARENTS—WHO ARE THEY, WHAT DO THEY WANT?

Main Focus: Understanding Mom and Dad's purposes and problems is often difficult for kids.

Biblical Basis: Deuteronomy 6:6, 7; Proverbs 4:3-5, 13:24; Matthew 20:20, 21; Hebrews 12:10, 11.

Materials Needed: One copy of the Teach 'Toon for every two or three students; scratch paper; pens or pencils; Bibles. OPTIONAL: A snack or other reward for the winner of the game in Step 1.

Before Class: Photocopy the Teach 'Toon. To save class time, you might want to write the things described in Step 3 on the chalkboard.

Step 1: This step is optional. If you'd like to start the lesson with a little fun, play a game of "Hangman" on the chalkboard. The word the students are looking for is *parents*. For an extra challenge, tell the students that you will scramble the order of the letters as you write them on the board. Give a reward to the one who guesses the word.

Explain that today's topic is parents and how to understand them.

Step 2: Distribute the Teach 'Toon copies, one to each group of two or three learners. Give the groups a few minutes to complete the Teach 'Toon.

Discuss what the groups have written. Ask the students to describe how they might behave if they were parents of a problem kid. Explain, **It's not easy to be a mom or a dad, even if you have great kids. Let's take a look at just a few things that parents are supposed to do—maybe this will help you understand what your parents go through with you.**

Step 3: List the five **Biblical Basis** passages in a column on the left side of the chalkboard. Write the following four phrases in a column on the right side: teach the Bible, seek God's favor for the kids, teach wise living, and discipline the kids.

Ask a volunteer to read the first passage. Have the class decide which phrase or phrases describe that passage. Draw a connecting line. Ask the students to relate specific instances when their moms or dads followed the passage's instructions. Ask, **Was it helpful to you when your mom or dad did this? Do you think it will be of help in the future? How? What would happen if your parents didn't do this? What about a kid whose parents aren't Christians? What disadvantages does he or she have?** Go over all the passages.

Step 4: Tell your class, **Work together in groups of three or four. I want each group to pretend it is devising a list of classes available at an imaginary university. The university teaches people how to be good parents. We'll call it Parents University or "PU" for short. First, figure out at least five or six things a person should know in order to be a good parent. Then take some paper and make a little book that lists each class with a short description. For example, you could have a class called "How to Listen to Your Kid's Side of the Story." The description could tell how it's important for parents and kids to communicate and to listen to each other.**

Encourage your students to think of topics like listening, trusting, spending time, awarding privileges, settling disagreements, money matters, and the four topics already mentioned.

As you discuss what your students come up with, be sure to ask them what the son or the daughter's responsibility is in regard to each area.

Step 5: Have your students work privately to write a "Treaty Between Me and Mom and Dad." In it, the student picks one area in which he or she will be more cooperative in order that mom or dad's job might be a bit easier this week. Explain that it is not necessary to show the treaty to their parents, but it would be nice if they did so.

Close in prayer.

GIVING IT AWAY

LOOK OVER THE VARIOUS WAYS CHRISTIANS ATTEMPT TO SHARE THEIR FAITH. THEN, LIST THEM IN THE ORDER OF WHICH YOU THINK THEY ARE THE MOST EFFECTIVE, #1 BEING THE BEST.

WHICH IS THE LEAST EFFECTIVE? WHY? WHICH IS THE MOST EFFECTIVE? WHY? WHICH WOULD YOU BE MOST LIKELY TO DO?

GIVING AWAY YOUR FAITH

Main Focus: Sharing our faith is more effective when it is done in genuine love.

Biblical Basis: Psalm 139:13, 14; John 1:12, 3:16, 14:6, 17:3; Romans 3:23; Ephesians 2:8, 9.

Materials Needed: Bibles; pens or pencils; a copy of the Teach 'Toon for each student; paper; index cards prepared as explained in **Before Class.**

Before Class: Photocopy the Teach 'Toon. Your students will perform a skit about a cure for cancer. Prepare a number of index cards as follows (make as many sets as you'll need for the number of small groups you expect to have):

> You have cancer and will probably die unless there is a cure. Ask for help.

> You have discovered the cure for cancer. Try to find as many cancer patients as you can for your cure.

> You are a doctor treating cancer patients. You do not believe there is a cure and you will forcefully block any suggestion that there is one.

> You have a family member who is a cancer patient. You want your loved one to get better, but you do not believe there is really a cure for cancer. You must discourage those who want to suggest there is a cure and keep them from your family member.

Step 1: Assemble your class into small groups. Give each group a prepared index card to secretly read. (If you have a small class, give a card to each student.) Explain that at your signal the groups are to mingle and do what is stated on their cards.

After several minutes call your groups together. Thank the students for their involvement and ask them to describe what occurred.

Tell your students that knowing Christ is almost like having the cure for cancer in a cancer ward—some people want to hear the message of the Gospel, while others are actively opposed to it.

Step 2: Hand out the Teach 'Toons and pens or pencils. Allow everyone to work individually. Each person is to put the examples of sharing the Christian faith in what they think is the proper order of effectiveness.

Have your students share which examples they feel to be the most effective and the least effective. Be sure they explain why they picked as they did. Tell the students to describe which of the methods they would be most likely to use.

Step 3: It is likely that your students will select methods that are more personal in nature, such as inviting people to church, sharing with them, or helping them out. In order to help your students know what essentials of the Christian message unbelievers need to hear, read the Scriptures under **Biblical Basis.** Distribute paper and ask the kids to restate in their own words the ideas they found in the Bible.

Step 4: Ask the young people to pick someone they know who needs to give his or her life to Christ. Spend some time in prayer for each of those people, then brainstorm ways the students might specifically make steps toward reaching out to their particular friends.